The Measurement of Corporate Environmental Activity

by

Loren A. Nikolai
John D. Bazley
R. Lee Brummet

Graduate School of Business Administration
University of North Carolina at Chapel Hill

National Association of Accountants
New York, N.Y.

Published by

National Association of Accountants
919 Third Avenue, New York, N.Y. 10022

Copyright by National Association of Accountants © 1976
Library of Congress Catalog Card Number 76-11662
NAA Publication Number 7684

Foreword

In the February 1974 issue of *Management Accounting*, the National Association of Accountants' Committee on Accounting for Corporate Social Performance released its first report, consisting of two parts. In the first part, the Committee stated objectives and procedures. In the second part, the Committee identified four major areas of social performance and listed typical examples within each area.

It is the stated objective of the Committee to develop systems of accounting for corporate social performance. In order to develop objective systems of measurement which may be used in assessing corporate social impact, the Committee called on the Association to sponsor a research program over several years. The research study whose findings are presented in this monograph is part of that program.

Guidance in the preparation of this monograph was provided by the Committee on Accounting for Corporate Social Performance:

I. Wayne Keller
Lancaster, Pennsylvania

Gregory J. Ahart
U.S. General Accounting Office
Washington, D.C.

Dennis R. Beresford
Ernst & Ernst
Cleveland, Ohio

R. Lee Brummet
University of North Carolina
Chapel Hill, North Carolina

Sidney Davidson
University of Chicago
Chicago, Illinois

Stan Hoch
General Electric Company
Fairfield, Connecticut

Stan M. Hunt
General Mills, Inc.
Minneapolis, Minnesota

Grant U. Meyers
Oil City Iron Works, Inc.
Corsicana, Texas

The monograph reflects the views of the researchers and not necessarily those of the Association or its committees.

Stephen Landekich
Research Director
National Association of Accountants

Preface

This research monograph focuses on one area of corporate social performance. It reports on corporate environmental activity, the measurement of such activity, and the resulting impact upon decision making. It is the culmination of a year-long study which included a questionnaire stage, an interview-case study stage, and an integration stage.

The overall objective of this research study is to provide a cohesive set of measurement techniques and information system modifications which might be used by corporations to evaluate their environmental impact. It is hoped that this study will aid in improving the quality of such measurements and, in so doing, assist companies in meeting their social responsibilities.

The authors wish to acknowledge the National Association of Accountants and its Committee on Accounting for Corporate Social Performance for their financial and institutional support. Appreciation is extended to Stephen Landekich, Research Director of the National Association of Accountants, for his advice and assistance in the completion of the research.

A special thanks is due to the companies which responded to the questionnaire and especially to the companies and executives who participated in the case studies. Without their assistance, the project would not have been possible.

Finally, appreciation is extended to Paul F. Williams for his timely and persistent library research, to all the secretaries who assisted us by typing various drafts of the monograph, and to the School of Business at the University of North Carolina for the use of its institutional facilities.

Loren A. Nikolai
John D. Bazley
R. Lee Brummet

TABLE OF CONTENTS

Chapter   Page

I. INTRODUCTION 1
    Methodology 1
        Questionnaire Stage 1
        Interview—Case Study Stage 2
        Integration Stage 2
    Overview of the Findings............................ 3
        Questionnaire Stage 3
        Interview—Case Study Stage 4
        Integration Stage 4
    Suggestions for Implementation...................... 6

II. MEASUREMENT OF ENVIRONMENTAL ACTIVITY:
    STATE OF THE ART 7
    General Information 9
    Costs Associated with Environmental Factors 10
        Additional Initial Costs...........................10
        Additional Operating Costs 10
        Additional Miscellaneous Costs 11
        Measurement of Costs............................11
        Reasons for Measuring the Costs 11
        Impact Upon Decision Making 14
        Reasons for Not Measuring the Costs 14
        Other Forms of Measurement 17
    Benefits Associated with Environmental Factors 17
        Reasons for Measuring the Benefits..................19
        Impact Upon Decision Making 19
        Reasons for Not Measuring the Benefits 21
        Other Forms of Measurement 21
    Further Analysis 21
    Summary and Conclusions 25

III. MEASUREMENT OF ENVIRONMENTAL ACTIVITY: CURRENT PRACTICES OF SELECTED COMPANIES ... 27
   Selection of Companies 27
   Format of Interviews 27
   The Case Studies 28
      Company A —Textiles 28
      Company B —Steel 30
      Company C —Paper Products 32
      Company D —Non-Ferrous Metals 34
      Company E —Food and Chemicals Manufacturing 36
      Company F —Tobacco 37
      Company G —Paper Products 39
      Company H —Non-Ferrous Metals 41
      Company I —Oil 43
   Summary and Conclusions 45

IV. RECOMMENDATIONS FOR MEASUREMENT AND DECISION MAKING CONCERNING ENVIRONMENTAL ACTIVITY 47
   Environmental Cost Definition 47
      Internal Revenue Service 48
      Council on Environmental Quality et. al. 49
      Department of Health, Education and Welfare 49
      The Conference Board 50
      The American Petroleum Institute 50
      Definition of Environmental Cost 52
   Environmental Cost Categories 54
      Initial Costs 54
      Operating Costs 55
      Exit Costs 57
      Environmental Cost Scorecard 57
   Environmental Benefits 57
      Internal Environmental Benefits 61
      External Environmental Benefits 63
   Planning 68
      Environmental Investments Planning 69
      Environmental Operational Planning and Control 80
   Summary and Conclusions 83

APPENDIX 85
BIBLIOGRAPHY 103

LIST OF EXHIBITS

Exhibit

Page

1. The Importance of Environmental Categories 9
2. The Importance of Functional Areas 10
3. The Monetary Measurement of Environmental Costs 12
4. Reasons Why Costs Are Measured In Monetary Terms 13
5. Impact of Monetary Cost Measurement on Decision Making . 15
6. Reasons Why Costs Are Not Measured In Monetary Terms .. 16
7. Non-Monetary Measurement of Environmental Costs 18
8. The Monetary Measurement of Environmental Benefits 19
9. Reasons Why Benefits Are Measured In Monetary Terms ... 20
10. Impact of Monetary Benefit Measurement on Decision Making 20
11. Reasons Why Benefits Are Not Measured In Monetary Terms 22
12. Non-Monetary Measurement of Environmental Benefits 23
13. The Effect of Commitment on the Measurement of Costs and Benefits 24
14. Air Pollution Abatement Installation—Electric Melt Shop ... 31
15. Environmental Cost Scorecard 58
16. Environmental Benefits Scorecard 60
17. Selected Water Quality Characteristics 65
18. General Rating Scale for the Quality Unit 67
19. Environmental Capital Investment Request 70
20. Selected Modifications of Capital Investment Analysis for Environmental Investments 74
21. The Analysis of Uncertain Factors in the Environmental Activity Decision 79

The Measurement of Corporate Environmental Activity

Chapter I
Introduction

Technology has been a major factor in raising the productivity of our economy and producing a high standard of living. Yet society is becoming increasingly aware of the side effects of technology in the areas of the environment and the conservation of scarce physical resources. Society is reflecting more concern for quality with quantity.

What effect has the concern of society for environmental impacts had upon the internal decision-making process of the firm? Do firms consider these impacts important enough to include them in their internal decision making as objectives or as constraints upon their objectives? If so, have they developed workable definitions and feasible measurements of these impacts, and have they been able to incorporate them adequately into their short-run and long-run decisions? Can the various methods by which some firms measure environmental impacts and incorporate such measurements into their information systems be synthesized into a set of normative adaptations which could be used by concerned firms? Finally, can these firms use this improved information in order to evaluate their ability to meet both their project objective as well as their social responsibility objective?

The purpose of this monograph is to report on a project designed to provide at least partial answers to these questions and problems and, in so doing, to provide a cohesive set of measurement techniques and information system modifications for use by corporations.

Methodology

The investigation was divided into three stages: 1) a questionnaire, 2) an interview-case study, and 3) an integration stage. The initiation of each of the later two stages was dependent upon successful completion of each prior stage.

Questionnaire Stage

Although society may view the consideration of environmental impacts as an attractive goal, firms may not agree that the measurement of these impacts should be incorporated into their internal decision-making process. Even if firms do desire to incorporate these measurements, they may not have developed a feasible way to do so. The purpose of the questionnaire stage was to ascertain the "state of the art" concerning the measurement techniques utilized to evaluate the costs and benefits associated with corporate actions which impact upon the environment and the resulting effect upon corporate decision making. These actions could be undertaken to meet legal requirements or to increase efficiency, but the questionnaire responses were restricted to the extent that such actions benefited the environment over and above meeting the basic economic needs of the company. In addition to determining whether certain costs and benefits were measured, the reasons why these measurements were or were not made were also ascertained. The results of the questionnaire stage are presented in Chapter II.

Interview–Case Study Stage

The purpose of the second stage of the project was to determine how companies are organized to make environmental decisions, how they measure the specific costs and benefits associated with these decisions, and how they incorporate such measurements into their planning and control processes.

Nine companies participated in this case study stage. These companies were chosen because of their apparent expertise in the environmental measurement area. The companies were selected so that the sample would cover a broad cross section of industry, including textiles, steel, paper, non-ferrous metals, food, chemicals, tobacco and oil.

Company personnel were queried about the ways in which responsibility and authority are delegated within their organizational structure and the make-up of the various environmental review committees. They were asked how an environmental expenditure is defined and which specific costs and benefits are measured. Further investigation was undertaken to determine the extent to which these measurements are expressed in monetary, quantitative but non-monetary, or narrative form. Finally, questions were directed towards determining how their planning models might be modified for environmental investments and what impact (if any) the related ongoing operating costs have upon their control function. The results of this interview–case study stage are presented in Chapter III.

Integration Stage

Many firms may reflect a social responsibility concerning their environmental activity, but some do not have the financial or personnel resources to adapt their information systems to include measurement of this activity. The integration stage was designed to review, synthesize and integrate the existing organizational structures, environmental definitions and measurement techniques along with the modifications of the information systems, as ascertained from the interview-case study stage in order to develop recommendations for measurement and decision making concerning environmental activity.

Specifically, the integration stage consisted of:

1) a review of the environmental literature specifically related to the objective,
2) an in-depth review of each firm's modifications of its measurement techniques and information systems,
3) an analysis of the similarities and differences between these modifications and those suggested or implied in the literature, and
4) an integration of these individual modifications into a set of "normative" definitions and suggestions concerning environmental measurement techniques and adaptations of information systems for use in internal decision making.

The results of this stage are presented in Chapter IV.

Overview of the Findings

Much information was gathered in each of the three stages of the project. A brief overview is presented here for the reader's convenience. For more detailed discussion on a specific stage of the project, the reader is directed to the applicable chapter.

Questionnaire Stage

The 95 companies which completed the questionnaire tend to be much more active in the measurement of the costs of environmental activities than of the benefits which accrue to them. This measurement activity is concentrated in the areas where traditional measurement techniques are applicable, such as environmental equipment costs and research and development costs. The primary reason for companies making these measurements is a desire to meet externally induced and self-imposed social responsibilities. Such measurements are considered to have an important impact upon company decision making.

Few of the responding companies measure their environmental activity in other than monetary terms. The companies which have an "environmental coordinator" generally are more active in their measurement activities than the companies without such a management position.

The most important reason for companies not to make particular environmental measurements is that they consider such measurements an undesirable use of monetary and personnel resources.

Interview-Case Study Stage

The companies which tend to be active in the environmental area are so because of a strong commitment and direction on the part of top management. Frequently these companies will have an environmental coordinator or committee to oversee such activities. In long-range environmental planning, engineers work with accounting personnel in the development of pollution control systems and in estimating costs. These costs usually are limited to equipment costs, primarily because of the absence of standard cost definitions. Very little measurement of benefits is made, although some narrative discussion of these benefits often is attached to capital investment request forms. Most of the companies attempt to comply with current pollution control standards but build into their systems sufficient flexibility so that modifications can be made when necessary. Traditional investment analysis methods tend to be utilized, but accept/reject criteria are likely to be modified to reflect the special characteristics of environmental projects.

When environmental projects go on-line, the associated capital costs generally are subsumed within typical plant and equipment categories. Certain companies separately measure and report ongoing pollution control operating costs, but this activity usually occurs when a separate operating unit for that purpose can be identified. No companies separately categorize environmental equipment depreciation, and few take advantage of the tax benefits to be derived from the pollution control facility accelerated amortization.

Integration Stage

The first two stages tend to be descriptive, while this final stage is intended to be prescriptive. In this stage, the nature of environmental costs and benefits is discussed along with their usefulness for the planning and control of environmental activities.

A definition of environmental costs is developed. It is concluded that environmental costs should include only the traceable incremental costs incurred for environmental activities.

Initial costs are categorized as land costs, equipment costs, engineering costs, research and development costs, and miscellaneous costs. Operating costs are classified as equipment operating costs, additional production costs, maintenance costs, disposal costs, monitoring costs, depreciation and miscellaneous costs. Finally, exit costs are identified primarily as restoration costs.

An environmental benefit is defined as a benefit to the environment which results from an expenditure of an environmental cost. Two types of environmental benefits are identified: 1) internal environmental benefits, which directly benefit the company while indirectly benefiting society; and 2) external environmental benefits, which directly benefit society while indirectly benefiting the company.

Internal environmental benefits are categorized as the use of recycled raw materials; the production of energy; the sale of by-products; the development of salable processes; the improvement of working conditions including reduced turnover, increased ability to attract new employees, reduced absenteeism and improved employee efficiency; and the improvement of the company's "good citizenship" reputation. Examples of external benefits include improvements in public water supply, recreational facilities, fish and wildlife support, vegetation, aesthetics and health. It is suggested that some sort of common "measurement unit" should be established in order to convey the relative impact of the company's activities upon these benefits.

Environmental investments planning, operational planning and control are discussed. A company environmental policy and environmental organizational structure are recommended. For environmental investments planning, an environmental capital investment request form is developed. This form includes sections for a description of the project, a summary of the non-monetary benefits, a summary of the annual monetary benefits and costs, a summary of the initial costs, and a presentation of the results from four different capital budgeting methods. It is suggested that environmental investments be evaluated as traditional capital investments, with certain modifications. Consideration should be given to Certified Pollution Control Facility acceleration amortization effects on cash flows, to savings in interest charges dues to financing via "pollution control bonds," to the evaluation of non-monetary benefits, and to the effect of changes in the values of the factors on the investment decision.

For operational planning, the authors recommend that the concept of responsibility accounting be extended to include environmental responsibility. In this way, the company can direct each manager's attention to the expected benefits received and costs incurred as a result of intended environmental activity for which he is responsible and which is undertaken to achieve the company's environmental social responsibility.

For control purposes, it is suggested that the company measure the actual costs incurred and the benefits obtained from environmental investments according to the categories discussed earlier. Modifications of normal control procedures are discussed, including environmental variance analyses and adjustments to performance evaluation.

Suggestions for Implementation

The overall objective of this research is to provide a cohesive set of measurement techniques and information system modifications which might be used by corporations to assess their environmental impact. The study represents an initial thrust into a measurement area which is recognized as being important, but also as being relatively underdeveloped and unsophisticated. It is hoped that this study achieves its objective and, to the extent that it does, improves the quality of such measurement.

Because of this underdevelopment, implementation of the suggestions contained herein is likely to be a somewhat lengthy, trial-and-error process. Nonetheless, the sooner the process is initiated, the sooner will be the improvements in such measurements. The authors recommend a sequential approach. A concerned company should begin by adopting an environmental policy statement and organizational structure similar to those suggested. Initially the company should focus upon the collection of cost data, using the suggested environmental cost definition and classification scheme, and the development of internal reporting with the suggested planning and control reports. Modifications of the definition and the classification and internal reporting schemes should be made to reflect particular company or industry differences or difficulties in implementation. A follow-up research study should be made with the assistance of companies which implement the suggestions in order to assess the usability of the suggestions and to make modifications, if necessary, to improve upon and refine the suggestions.

Once a company has an operable environmental-cost information system, it should direct its attention to the quantification of environmental benefits. This measurement area is the least developed and, consequently, will require the most effort and time for improvement. A two-pronged approach may accelerate this process. First, a company should devote significant resources to identifying all of the internal and external environmental benefits. It should call upon its accounting, engineering and scientific personnel to utilize their expertise to devise innovative methods of quantification so that a common environmental benefit "measurement unit" may evolve. The successes and failures in this area should be exchanged freely via trade associations, industry journals and other media so that collective corporate expertise can be marshalled effectively. Second, interdisciplinary academic research should be undertaken. This research should combine specific company or industry models in order to develop more generalized environmental benefit measurement models. Only through a continuing liaison between industry and academia will rapid and significant environmental benefit measurement improvements be achieved.

Chapter II
Measurement of Environmental Activity: State of the Art

The purpose of the questionnaire stage was to investigate the desirability and feasibility of environmental measurements. The questionnaire was designed to determine the kinds of measurements utilized by each company to evaluate the costs and benefits associated with corporate actions which impact upon the environment and the resulting effect upon corporate decision making.

The questionnaire was divided into several sections: 1) an introduction; 2) Part I, which elicited general information; 3) Part II, which was concerned with the costs associated with environmental factors; and 4) Part III, which was concerned with the benefits associated with environmental factors. A copy of the questionnaire is presented in the Appendix.

The introduction was designed to clarify certain information for the respondent. The purpose of the questionnaire was explained, and the NAA sponsorship was noted. It was explained that:

1) "environmental factors" referred to such aspects as air, water, and land pollution; aesthetics; and the consumption, recycling, or disposal of non-replaceable physical resources;

2) the questionnaire was concerned with corporate actions impacting upon the environment, whether or not they were undertaken to meet legal requirements or to increase efficiency, but only to the extent such actions benefit the environment over and above meeting the basic economic needs of the company;

3) the questionnaire should be completed by an individual who is both knowledgeable of corporate efforts to measure relevant costs and benefits associated with environmental factors and in a position to judge the impact of such measurements on company decision making; and

4) the questionnaire should be completed for the company as a whole (or relevant "segment" thereof) plus any domestic subsidiaries.

Finally, the respondents were assured that their responses would be confidential and that a copy of the results would be furnished to those interested.

Part I, titled "General Information," included questions concerning the rank within each organization of the highest executive who deals primarily with measuring the costs and benefits associated with environmental matters, the degree to which costs associated with each major type of pollution are measured, and the significance of the contribution made by each functional area of the company to the measurement of costs and benefits associated with environmental factors.

Part II, titled "Costs Associated with Environmental Factors," was separated into three sub-sections dealing with additional initial costs, additional operating costs, and additional miscellaneous costs. The "Additional Initial Costs" section included the measurement and separate classification of such costs as research and development, equipment, disruption, and legal costs. The "Additional Operating Costs" section included such costs as production, monitoring, recycling, avoidance, disposal, and maintenance costs. The "Additional Miscellaneous Costs" section included such costs as aesthetic, restoration, and image promotion costs.

Part III, titled "Benefits Associated with Environmental Factors," was concerned with the additional benefits derived and separately categorized as a result of a concern with the effect of each company's planned or actual activities upon environmental factors. These benefits included reduced production costs, avoidance of legal costs and penalties, the reduction in pollution caused by the company's activities or products, and the conservation of scarce physical resources.

Each cost section and the benefit section consisted of five questions. The questions were designed so they could be answered by a respondent placing a check mark or a number on the appropriate line. The questions included whether or not the company measured, in monetary terms, the specific additional costs (or benefits); if so, why they measured such costs (or benefits) and what impact these measurements had upon their decision making; and if not, why they did not measure such costs (or benefits) and whether these items were measured in other than monetary terms.

The questionnaire, along with a cover letter, was sent to 984 of the *Fortune* "top 1,000" industrial corporations. Ninety-five corporations from a cross section of industries completed the questionnaire.

General Information

The purpose of the initial section of the questionnaire was to determine certain general information about the respondents. The first question asked if there exists in the organization an individual who has as a major portion of his/her responsibility a concern with the measurement of the costs and benefits associated with environmental factors and the resulting effect upon corporate decision making. It also was asked whether such an individual is a corporate vice president or above. Twenty-two percent of those firms responding reported that they have a corporate vice president or above, 26 percent that they have a person below corporate vice president, and 52 percent that they do not have a member of the organization who has a concern with costs and benefits of environmental factors as a major portion of his/her responsibility.

The two other general items that were investigated were the particular environmental categories that are of concern to the respondents and the degree to which the various functional areas contribute to the company's measurement activities. The percentage of the respondents who measure the costs associated with particular environmental categories to a major or moderate degree is shown in Exhibit 1.

EXHIBIT 1

THE IMPORTANCE OF ENVIRONMENTAL CATEGORIES

Percentage of Responding Companies that Measure Costs
Associated with Each Environmental Category to a
Major or Moderate Degree

Environmental Category	Percentage
Water	72
Air	70
Land	37
Noise	52
Other (including solid waste disposal)	13

The significance of the contribution that each functional area has made as the company has progressed in its attempts to make measurements, in monetary terms, of the costs and benefits associated with environmental factors is shown in Exhibit 2. Again, the percentage of respondents who indicated that the area had made a major or moderate contribution is shown in the exhibit.

EXHIBIT 2

THE IMPORTANCE OF FUNCTIONAL AREAS

Percentage of Responding Companies Indicating Major or Moderate Contributions Made by Functional Areas to Their Environmental Measurement Activity

Functional Area	Percentage
Manufacturing	61
Engineering	70
Research & Development	41
Legal	20
Accounting	43
Marketing	9

Costs Associated with Environmental Factors

Part II of the questionnaire was concerned with costs incurred and categorized separately because of a concern with the effect of the company's planned or actual activities upon environmental factors. The costs were divided into three categories: additional initial costs, additional operating costs, and additional miscellaneous costs.

Additional Initial Costs

Four categories of additional initial costs were identified as 1) research and development costs; 2) equipment costs, including capital asset, installation and testing costs; 3) disruption costs, including additional opportunity costs and any "down-time" costs; and 4) legal costs.

Additional Operating Costs

Six categories of additional operating costs were identified as 1) production costs, including additional materials, direct labor, and direct overhead; 2) monitoring costs, including additional costs of labor, supplies, and others to monitor the degree of compliance with predetermined acceptable levels of pollution; 3) recycling costs, including additional costs incurred as a result of recycling physical resources; 4) avoidance costs, including the costs of preparing (or purifying) a polluted natural resource used as an input into the production process; 5) disposal costs, including costs incurred that are associated with the adequate disposal of waste products which are not recycled; and 6) maintenance costs, including costs of labor, supplies, and such to keep the pollution control equipment functioning properly.

Additional Miscellaneous Costs

Three categories of additional miscellaneous costs were identified as 1) aesthetic costs, incurred to design, locate, and maintain facilities in conformance with aesthetically pleasing architecture and landscaping; 2) restoration costs, including additional costs incurred to restore voluntarily the removal site of the natural resource to an environmentally satisfactory state; and 3) image promotion costs, including costs incurred to communicate a realistic and positive image of environmental concern of the company. There was also a category for "other" additional miscellaneous costs.

Measurement of Costs

The first question for each category of costs was whether the company measures in monetary terms the additional costs associated with the effect of that company's planned or actual activities upon environmental factors. The respondents' answers to this question are summarized in Exhibit 3.

Reasons for Measuring the Costs

The questionnaire also was designed to determine for those companies which do measure costs the reasons why they measure in monetary terms each category of additional costs. The respondents were asked to evaluate the impact that each of five reasons has on their decision to undertake the cost measurements (an "other" category also was available). Four possible responses for each reason were allowed by the format of the question: no impact, minor impact moderate impact, major impact. The percentage of the respondents who measure each type of cost and who consider each reason to be of major or moderate impact on their decision to undertake the cost measurements is shown in Exhibit 4. The responses to the questionnaire indicate that the two most important reasons for undertaking the measurement of environmental costs is for decision making concerning both self-imposed and externally induced social responsibilities. Generally, neither reason is clearly more important than the other, except in the case of the measurement of additional miscellaneous costs where the self-imposed social responsibilities appear to be more important than those that are externally induced.

The next most important reason for monetary measurement is for a firm to meet legal requirements (with expenditures on equipment being the most important category). For example, expenditures to meet pollution control laws would be included in this category, as opposed to voluntary expenditures to control pollution which would have been included in one of the "social responsibility" categories. Also, it can be seen from Ex-

EXHIBIT 3

THE MONETARY MEASUREMENT OF ENVIRONMENTAL COSTS

Percentage of Responding Companies that Measure
Specific Additional Environmental Costs in
Monetary Terms

Costs	**Percentage**
A. Additional Initial Costs	
Research & Development	62
Equipment	93
Disruption	37
Legal	34
B. Additional Operating Costs	
Production	61
Monitoring	54
Recycling	39
Avoidance	31
Disposal	66
Maintenance	66
C. Additional Miscellaneous Costs	
Aesthetic	22
Restoration	25
Image Promotion	18

EXHIBIT 4

REASONS WHY COSTS ARE MEASURED IN MONETARY TERMS

Percentage of Responding Companies Indicating
Major or Moderate Reason

Costs	To Meet Legal Requirements	For External Reporting	To Obtain Pollution Control Tax Advantages	For Decision Making Concerning Self-Imposed Social Responsibilities	For Decision Making Concerning Externally Induced Social Responsibilities
A. Additional Initial Costs					
Research & Development	40	27	12	54	50
Equipment	62	41	44	59	55
Disruption	22	31	19	61	53
Legal	54	32	17	40	45
B. Additional Operating Costs					
Production	34	33	24	54	55
Monitoring	49	41	21	57	62
Recycling	25	24	22	57	53
Avoidance	42	19	19	65	60
Disposal	28	32	16	53	57
Maintenance	27	28	13	50	51
C. Additional Miscellaneous Costs					
Aesthetic	5	30	5	100	58
Restoration	44	30	13	71	48
Image Promotion	19	33	6	75	53

hibit 4 that external reporting requirements are relatively unimportant, which is not surprising since there are no enforceable requirements to report costs. The Securities and Exchange Commission, however, does require disclosure of the effects of compliance with environmental laws in various reports filed with it. Of course, many companies voluntarily include the costs of meeting environmental requirements in external reports, but this is on an unaudited "public relations" basis. It also appears that comparatively few companies are taking advantage of the pollution control tax advantages that can be obtained.

Impact Upon Decision Making

The respondents were asked to evaluate the impact that these cost measurements have upon company decision making. The percentage of respondents who measure in monetary terms each category of costs and who consider the impact on decision making to be of major or moderate significance is reported in Exhibit 5. The percentages generally are high, which is to be expected because companies that do take the trouble to categorize and measure the costs of environmental factors can be expected to use them in their decision making. Only five percent of the respondents indicated that the measurement of the costs has no impact on decision making.

Some reasons can be suggested concerning why some companies make such monetary measurements but consider them to have little effect on decision making. Companies may be concerned about the reliability of their numbers, the costs may include a large proportion of allocated costs, or the costs may be small compared to the other costs involved in their decisions.

Reasons for Not Measuring the Costs

The respondents who do not measure in monetary terms the additional costs associated with environmental factors were asked for the reasons why such measurements are not made. The format of the question was the same as that of the reasons for measuring costs. The percentage of the respondents who do not measure each type of cost and who consider each reason to have a major or moderate impact on their decision not to undertake such measurements is shown in Exhibit 6. The two most important reasons for not undertaking measurements is that it is not considered a desirable use of financial or of personnel resources, with the lack of personnel resources generally considered more important. The fact that measurements are not legally required has a significant influence on the absence of cost measurements. The relatively small percentage of respondents who indicated that they felt constrained by the lack of techniques

EXHIBIT 5

IMPACT OF MONETARY COST MEASUREMENT ON DECISION MAKING

Percentage of Responding Companies Indicating
Major or Moderate Impact

Costs	**Percentage**
A. Additional Initial Costs	
Research and Development	61
Equipment	85
Disruption	61
Legal	50
B. Additional Operating Costs	
Production	82
Monitoring	52
Recycling	63
Avoidance	71
Disposal	70
Maintenance	73
C. Additional Miscellaneous Costs	
Aesthetic	72
Restoration	70
Image Promotion	63

EXHIBIT 6

REASONS WHY COSTS ARE NOT MEASURED IN MONETARY TERMS

Percentage of Responding Companies Indicating
Major or Moderate Reason

Costs	Not Required Legally	Not Desirable Use of Monetary Resources	Not Desirable Use of Personnel Resources	No Monetary Resources To Do So	No Personnel Resources To Do So	No Techniques Available
A. Additional Initial Costs						
Research & Development	32	47	63	6	16	32
Equipment	50	60	67	0	0	29
Disruption	34	44	64	4	11	21
Legal	37	42	53	3	6	18
B. Additional Operating Costs						
Production	35	57	63	6	13	19
Monitoring	33	49	54	8	10	15
Recycling	36	55	64	8	10	15
Avoidance	30	52	53	3	8	18
Disposal	25	54	55	4	4	14
Maintenance	26	52	54	4	7	12
C. Additional Miscellaneous Costs						
Aesthetic	28	52	52	7	6	21
Restoration	25	47	46	7	5	19
Image Promotion	26	52	54	6	7	17

available should be interpreted with caution since these are respondents who do not make measurements and, therefore, may not become aware of the difficulty in making the measurements until they attempt them. Few companies admitted that they do not have the financial or personnel resources available, which is not surprising in view of the large size of each responding company.

Other Forms of Measurement

Since the previous questions dealt with monetary measurement, the respondents who do not make such measurements were asked if they measure those items in another quantitative or non-quantitative manner. The percentage of the respondents who do not measure the items in monetary form (as costs) but who undertake measurements in quantitative (but not dollar) terms or who make non-quantitative measurements is shown in Exhibit 7. It can be seen clearly that few companies measure these factors in any way other than in monetary terms; i.e., the vast majority either measured costs in monetary terms or made no measurements at all. This result supports the view that accountants do have a significant role to play in the evluation by companies of environmental factors.

Benefits Associated With Environmental Factors

In Part III of the questionnaire, the respondents were asked to answer five questions which dealt specifically with the additional benefits that accrue to the company (as opposed to society) and which are measured and categorized separately as a result of a concern with the effect of the company's planned or actual activities upon environmental factors. Seven types of benefits were identified as: 1) reduced production costs, 2) avoidance of legal costs and penalties, 3) improved public image, 4) improved employee satisfaction, 5) reduction in pollution caused by the company's activities, 6) reduction in pollution caused by the use of the company's products, and 7) conservation of scarce physical resources (including either reduced use or recycling).

In the first question, the respondents were asked if their company measures, in monetary terms, each of the seven benefits. The results are summarized in Exhibit 8.

It may be seen that the responding companies, in general, do not measure environmental benefits in monetary terms. The benefits that are measured most often are reduced production costs and conservation of scarce physical resources. The probable reason for the measurement of reduced production costs is that this measurement would use techniques developed from traditional measurement activity. It is likely that the conservation of scarce physical resources is the category of benefits that probably has had the most recent public impact. Two other benefits are

EXHIBIT 7

NON-MONETARY MEASUREMENT OF ENVIRONMENTAL COSTS

Percentage of Responding Companies that Make Non-Monetary Measurements of Cost

Costs	Quantitative (Non-Monetary)	Non Quantitative
A. Additional Initial Costs		
Research & Development	0	18
Equipment	14	0
Disruption	9	11
Legal	5	12
B. Additional Operating Costs		
Production	3	0
Monitoring	5	12
Recycling	2	11
Avoidance	2	6
Disposal	6	0
Maintenance	3	3
C. Additional Miscellaneous Costs		
Aesthetic	0	20
Restoration	2	8
Image Promotion	0	19

EXHIBIT 8

THE MONETARY MEASUREMENT OF ENVIRONMENTAL BENEFITS

Percentage of Responding Companies that Measure
Specific Additional Environmental Benefits
in Monetary Terms

Benefits	Percentage
Reduced Production Costs	48
Avoid Legal Costs	27
Improved Public Image	11
Improved Employee Satisfaction	11
Reduced Pollution by Company	33
Reduced Pollution by Product	14
Conservation of Physical Resources	44

measured to a lesser extent—the reduction in pollution caused by the company's activities and the avoidance of legal costs or penalties. The other three benefits essentially are not measured.

Reasons for Measuring the Benefits

The second question examined the reasons why those companies which measure each of the seven benefits in monetary terms make such measurements. The responses to this question are summarized in Exhibit 9. This exhibit is limited to the four benefits which respondents indicated in the previous question that they measure to a significant degree.

A review of Exhibit 9 indicates that the primary reason for measuring both reduced production costs and the conservation of scarce physical resources is for decision making concerning self-imposed social responsibilities, with externally induced social responsibilities being nearly as important. The primary reason for measuring the reduction in pollution caused by the company's activities and the avoidance of legal costs and penalties is to meet legal requirements. For each of these benefits, with the exception of the reduction in pollution caused by the company's activities, the remaining reasons tend to be far less important. For this latter benefit, all of the reasons tend to be important.

Impact Upon Decision Making

The respondents next were asked to indicate the impact these benefits measurements have upon the company's decision making. A summary of these responses is presented in Exhibit 10. Again, this exhibit is limited to the four benefits which are measured to a significant degree.

EXHIBIT 9

REASONS WHY BENEFITS ARE MEASURED IN MONETARY TERMS

Percentage of Responding Companies Indicating Major
or Moderate Reason

	Reduced Production Cost	Avoid Legal Cost	Reduced Pollution By Company	Conserve Physical Resources
Reasons:				
To provide information:				
To meet legal requirements	21	76	65	12
For external reporting	16	17	46	26
To obtain pollution control tax advantages	7	8	26	7
For decision making concerning self-imposed social responsibilities	49	46	67	66
For decision making concerning externally induced social responsibilities	30	42	54	39

EXHIBIT 10

IMPACT OF MONETARY BENEFIT MEASUREMENT ON DECISION MAKING

Percentage of Responding Companies Indicating Major
or Moderate Impact

Benefits	Percentage
Reduced Production Costs	88
Avoidance of Legal Costs	75
Reduced Pollution by Company	82
Conservation of Physical Resources	84

The percentages generally are high, which is to be expected, because companies that take the trouble to categorize and measure in monetary terms the benefits derived from environmental activities can be expected to use them in their decision making.

Consistent with the previous findings, the two benefits which are measured most often in monetary terms—reduced production costs and the conservation of scarce physical resources—also have the most impact upon company decision making. Other benefits have almost as significant an impact on decision making, whereas the cost measurements do not have such a consistent impact on decision making.

Reasons for Not Measuring the Benefits

Two additional questions were asked for any of the benefits not measured in monetary terms. One was designed to determine the reasons why the benefits are not measured in monetary terms. The answers to this question are summarized in Exhibit 11.

The reasons "not desirable use of monetary resources" and "not desirable use of personal resources" are cited most often for not measuring the benefits in monetary terms. Generally the companies report that there are fewer techniques available for measuring benefits than for costs.

Other Forms of Measurements

The last question in this section asked the respondents to indicate, for those benefits not measured in monetary terms, if and how the companies do measure these benefits. A summary of these responses is presented in Exhibit 12.

It is apparent from the exhibit that, while a few companies attempt to aggregate non-quantitative information concerning these benefits, most companies do not measure them.

Further Analysis

The questionnaire was concerned primarily with determining the degree to which companies measure the costs and benefits associated with environmental factors and the reasons why those particular measurements are or are not made. However, although not a primary goal in the use of the questionnaire, it is also of interest to attempt to determine if there are particular characteristics of companies that lead them to to get involved in the measurement process.

As reported earlier, the respondents were asked if there exists in the organization a person who has as a major portion of his/her responsibility, a concern with the measurement of the costs and benefits associated with environmental factors. The answer to this question can be taken as

EXHIBIT 11

REASONS WHY BENEFITS ARE NOT MEASURED IN MONETARY TERMS

Percentage of Responding Companies Indicating Major or Moderate Reason

Reasons:	Reduced Production Cost	Avoid Legal Cost	Improve Public Image	Improve Employee Satisfaction	Reduced Pollution By Company	Reduced Pollution By Product	Conserve Physical Resources
Not required legally	33	27	25	25	32	28	28
Not desirable use of monetary resources	54	58	56	54	55	50	52
Not desirable use of personnel resources	53	60	53	49	50	46	52
No monetary resources to do so	9	8	5	5	5	4	6
No personnel resources to do so	12	10	7	7	7	4	7
No techniques available to do so	25	20	30	33	24	28	24

EXHIBIT 12

NON-MONETARY MEASUREMENT OF ENVIRONMENTAL BENEFITS

Percentage of Responding Companies that Make
Non-Monetary Measurements of Benefits

Benefits:	Quantitative (Non-Monetary)	Non Quantitative
Reduced production costs	6	11
Avoidance of legal costs and penalties	3	15
Improved public image	1	29
Improved employee satisfaction	1	34
Reduction in pollution caused by the company's activities	15	25
Reduction in pollution caused by the use of the company's products	6	12
Conservation of scarce physical resources	7	23

an indication of a degree of "commitment" made by a company. However, it must be emphasized that a question did refer specifically to the measurement of costs and benefits and thus is examining a specialized kind of commitment.

It does not necessarily follow that "committed" companies (those answering "yes" to the above question) are more active in measuring costs and benefits. Therefore, it was decided to determine whether committed companies are more successful in the implementation of the measurement techniques than the non-committed companies. A comparison was made between these two groups of companies regarding the types of costs and benefits which each measure. The results of this analysis are reported in Exhibit 13.

For every category of costs and benefits, the committed companies are more active in terms of the degree of measurement activity undertaken, and in 16 of the 20 categories the difference is statistically significant.

Another indication of the degree of activity undertaken is provided by the responses to the question concerning whether companies make quantitative or non-quantitative measurements, given that they do not measure dollar amounts of the costs and benefits. The committed companies gene-

EXHIBIT 13

THE EFFECT OF COMMITMENT ON THE MEASUREMENT OF COSTS AND BENEFITS

Percentages of Committed and Non-Committed Companies that Measure Costs and Benefits

Costs	Committed Companies	Non-Committed Companies
A. Additional Initial Costs		
Research & Development	76	49**
Equipment	100	86*
Disruption	54	21**
Legal	46	22*
B. Additional Operating Costs		
Production	76	47**
Monitoring	76	35**
Recycling	55	23**
Avoidance	41	20*
Disposal	80	53**
Maintenance	78	55*
C. Additional Indirect Costs		
Aesthetic	29	15
Restoration	41	10**
Image Promotion	26	10*
D. Additional Benefits		
Reduced Production Costs	67	31**
Avoid Legal Costs	43	12**
Improved Public Image	15	6
Improved Employee Satisfaction	15	6
Reduced Pollution by Company	50	16**
Reduced Pollution by Product	20	8
Conservation of Physical Resources	61	29**

**Difference is significant at the .01 level.   *Difference is significant at the .05 level.

rally make more of these non-dollar measurements, especially for those categories in which relatively little dollar measurement takes place.

Summary and Conclusions

The questionnaire was used to learn about the interest and practices of companies in measuring the costs and benefits associated with their actions which impact upon the environment. In addition, the reasons why measurements are or are not made was investigated, along with the effect of such measurements upon corporate decision making.

Generally the responding companies are much more active in the monetary measurement of the costs of environmental factors than they are of the benefits which accrue to them. Furthermore, measurement activity appears to be concentrated in the areas where traditional measurement techniques can be utilized most easily, such as equipment costs and research and development costs as opposed to aesthetic and image-promotion costs.

The most significant reasons why companies undertake monetary measurements are because of a desire to meet externally induced and self-imposed social responsibilities. These general reasons are more important than the more specific reasons of meeting legal requirements, obtaining tax advantages, or meeting external reporting requirements.

As would be expected, those companies that measure the costs and benefits of environmental factors generally consider that they have an important effect on their decision making.

The most important reasons why companies do not measure costs and benefits in monetary terms are because they consider such measurement to be an undesirable use of financial and personnel resources rather than because there is a lack of techniques available. Of course, those who do not measure may be unaware of the difficulty of doing so. A considerable number of the companies do not make the measurements because they are not required by law to do so. Very few companies consider a lack of personnel or financial resources as reasons for not measuring, which is to be expected because of the large size of each responding company.

Very few companies measure any of the environmental factors in other than dollar terms. Apparently few other forms of quantitative measurement or even non-quantitative measurement are utilized. This suggests that accountants do have a significant role to play in the evaluation by companies of environmental factors.

It also was found that committed companies (determined by whether there exists in the company a person who has a major portion of his/her responsibility a concern with the measurement of the costs and benefits associated with environmental factors) are more active in their measurement activity than the remaining non-committed companies.

Chapter III
Measurement of Environmental Activity: Current Practices of Selected Companies

The purpose of this second stage of the research was to determine how selected firms measure specific environmental factors and how they incorporate them into their information systems and decision making.

Selection of Companies

In the questionnaire, companies were asked if they were willing to participate in the second stage of the project. Several companies responded that they were willing to participate. Two basic criteria were used to select companies from those willing to participate. First, their responses to the questionnaire had to indicate that they were undertaking a significant amount of environmental measurement of a reasonably sophisticated nature. Second, a sample of companies which covered a broad cross section of industry was considered desirable. The process described did not achieve a sufficiently broad cross section, so contacts were made with additional companies in order to achieve the desired coverage.

Nine companies participated in this stage of the research. The industries covered were textiles, steel, paper, non-ferrous metals, food, chemicals, tobacco and oil. Seven of the nine companies are in the *Fortune* 500.

Format of Interviews

Interviews were conducted with several officers of each firm. The officers were primarily accountants and environmental engineers.

A general format was followed for each interview. First, the organization of the company for decision making in the environmental area was discussed, along with the company activities which cause the greatest environmental problems. Since environmental problems are so widespread and large companies have such diversified activities, the discussion usually concentrated on a few selected activities which the company considered to be the most important and relevant.

The discussion of the monetary measurement of costs and benefits concentrated on the categories of items which are measured by the company, the specific measurements which are included in each category, the problems involved in categorizing items as environmental or non-environmental, and whether their measurement consists solely of estimating costs for planning purposes or includes the measurement of actual costs. The types of non-monetary measurement made by the company also were discussed, along with the problems of converting such items into monetary measurement. The degree to which environmental items are categorized separately in the reports produced for management also was examined.

The Case Studies

Summaries of the nine case studies which were conducted follow. These summaries are not intended to include all the information which was obtained from each company but to give the reader an indication of the variety of problems faced by each company and the variety of solutions and measurements used.

Company A—Textiles

Organizational Structure and Environmental Problems

Company A is a textile company which is organized on a divisional basis according to its various production activities. This structure has resulted in a situation in which the staff functions have significantly less power than the production-oriented divisions. Therefore, ultimate responsibility for environmental activities clearly lies with the managers of the production divisions although assistance is provided by the staff functions for the identification of the various pollution control requirements and satisfying such requirements.

The company has two major pollution problems—water and air. Water is used in the production process and becomes contaminated with various chemicals such as dyes, starches, bleaches and chrome. These pollutants generally are removed from the water in settling ponds, although in a few cases the effluent is pumped into the local municipal sewage system. However, since the municipality charges on the basis of the contents of the sewage as well as the volume, it is not necessarily a less expensive alternative. In some situations it may be advantageous for the company to remove a pollutant by using substitute chemicals in the production process rather than by cleaning the waste water. Generally the company has no problem with the cleanliness of the input water (which is obtained primarily from company-owned sources), and there is little recycling of water at the present time.

The company has a minor external air pollution problem which results from heating with oil, coal or natural gas. There was a more serious air pollution problem within the various plants because particulate matter (especially cotton) was present in the air. A two-pronged approach was used to solve the problem. A chute-fed carding system was installed to help prevent the particulate matter from escaping into the air, and air conditioning was installed to help remove the particles that did escape into the air.

The company also has a problem with noise from machinery which is currently being mitigated by issuing ear plugs to the employees.

The company has an interesting interaction problem. After removing the pollutants from the water at one of its plants, it is unable to dispose of the resulting sludge because of strict land pollution laws. The current solution to the problem is to give it to the local municipality which is able to burn it because the municipality is subject to less strict laws than the company.

Measurement Activity

The company's measurement of initial costs is centered primarily on equipment costs. Although not categorized specifically as environmental costs, the costs are categorized in a sufficiently precise manner so that a special review could identify such costs. Generally a project is considered by the company to be either entirely environmental or not at all environmental. This arises partly from the nature of the projects they have undertaken and partly because of the acknowledged difficulty of separating individual costs of the components of the project if they have economic benefits as well as environmental benefits. For example, the equipment installed to solve the internal air pollution problem also will improve employee satisfaction, reduce employee absenteeism, reduce employee turnover and hence hiring costs, attract labor in order to utilize idle machines, reduce production costs because of improved employee and machine efficiency, and improve the quality of the product. However, there are obvious difficulties in measuring these benefits, and the company has not attempted to do so although they are convinced that such benefits are realized. Likewise all the costs of the equipment are considered to be environmental because of the difficulty of determining which parts of the total expenditure have economic benefits to the company and which result solely in reduced pollution.

There was no significant interruption of production when the pollution control equipment was installed, so disruption costs have not been measured. Research and development expenditures for environmental factors can be identified readily because of the structure of the R & D division in which environmental R & D is separated from the other activities.

Limited measurement of operating costs is undertaken. The costs of operating the water pollution equipment which is specific to a single plant are categorized as labor, chemicals, and repair and maintenance and are charged to the production manager's budget although it is acknowledged that there is limited controllability. Some of the plants also are charged on a gallons-used basis for the costs of a waste treatment facility which is common to several plants. Depreciation of pollution control equipment is not categorized separately.

The company has incurred some aesthetic costs, such as the cost of installing aluminum siding on an unattractive building, but it does not consider such costs to be environmental.

Company B—Steel

Organization Structure and Environmental Problems

Company B is a steel company which primarily produces special purpose steels. Its major environmental problem is air pollution, with water pollution being of secondary importance. The air pollution problem is caused by the use of furnaces. Originally the company used only open hearth furnaces, some of which currently are operating under a variance from the State Pollution Control Board. Some years ago, several of the open hearth furnaces were replaced by electric furnaces for economic reasons, but replacements now are being considered for environmental reasons. The electric furnaces which originally were installed had to be modified to meet current laws, but the latest furnace was designed to satisfy the legal requirements immediately.

Measurement Activity

The capital costs of the pollution control equipment are identified, which presents few problems because the equipment, such as duct work and bag houses, is physically separate. One of the major motivations for the separate identification of these costs is to satisfy the requirements of pollution control bonds which the company uses for financing the pollution control equipment.

Research and development and internal engineering costs are expensed with no attempt made to categorize the environmental expenditures.

An example of the expenditures made on a particular pollution control installation (expressed in percentages so as to maintain confidentiality) is shown in Exhibit 14. The engineering expense results from contracts with other companies and therefore can be measured and categorized readily.

EXHIBIT 14

AIR POLLUTION ABATEMENT INSTALLATION-ELECTRIC MELT SHOP

	Estimated % of Cost
1. Site Preparation Including Roadways and Grading	.4
2. Purchase of Fume Control Equipment	34.8
3. Installation of Fume Control Equipment Including Foundations	24.3
4. Electrical Feeders and Substation	7.3
5. Water Cooling System	6.7
6. Modification to existing "A" & "B" Collection Systems	2.1
7. Purchase & Installation of Related Facilities such as Personnel Elevator, Crane for Alloy Charging Bay and Gravity Roof Ventilations	4.5
8. Moving and Relocations	2.1
9. Premium Time	2.1
10. Engineering Expense	8.4
11. Recommended Spares	2.0
12. Contingencies & Escalation Allowance	5.3

The company is in the process of identifying some of the operating costs associated with its pollution control activities. A list of expense codes is shown below:

Repair and Maintenance Labor—Pollution Equipment
Preventive Maintenance Labor—Pollution Equipment
Repair and Maintenance Material—Pollution Equipment
Repair and Maintenance Outside—Pollution Equipment
Other Material—Pollution Equipment
Other Labor and Material Outside—Pollution Equipment

Some of the operating costs that are not categorized separately are very significant. The costs of monitoring and operating the pollution abatement equipment used with the electric furnaces are not identified even though these annual costs amount to approximately 20 percent of the total capital expenditures.

In addition, the pollution control equipment does increase operating costs even when it is operating perfectly. However, it often is not working at optimum efficiency, in which case the effect on costs may become significant. For example, if the equipment is withdrawing too much air, then more heat is needed for the furnace, which wears out the carbon electrodes in the furnace faster, the process takes longer, and the quality of the steel is lower. The company management does not feel that it is practical to attempt to isolate these additional costs, although it is believed that if the company were allowed to violate pollution control laws temporarily, an experiment conducted for eight hours per day for two weeks could give a very good indication of these additional production costs associated with the equipment. The experiment would involve running with and without the pollution control equipment.

A potential benefit is that the bag houses collect the particulate matter which includes valuable minerals, although they are not salable in their present form.

The primary benefit of the pollution control equipment is the avoidance of legal penalties and the ability to stay in business. For example, if the open hearth furnaces are closed down, 200 jobs would be lost, in addition to the lost sales. A special problem is caused by the fact that the state environmental department legally is not allowed to consider the economic effects of complying with pollution control laws.

Other minor benefits are that the reduced smoke from the furnaces improves the operating efficiency of crane operators and also extends the life of electric installations in the roof.

One behavioral problem that arises with respect to the operation of the pollution control equipment is that the production managers could improve their efficiency if the equipment were not operating. Therefore, the management considers it advantageous to isolate the employees who operate the pollution control equipment so that they will be less likely to be subject to undue pressure from the production managers.

The water pollution problem is relatively minor, but the company does have a recycling process in effect at one of its new plants. This is necessary because the flow of the water in the river is insufficient for the needs of the plant. The water in the river is controlled by a river authority which has instituted a charge for water used in excess of historical amounts. This charge could be used as the basis for determining the opportunity cost associated with recycling although the company has not considered it in that manner.

Company C—Paper Products

Organizational Structure and Environmental Problems

Company C is a paper products company which produces high-quality specialty pulp. The company has an environmental engineering department which is responsible to the director of corporate engineering. The typical process followed in the analysis of a pollution control expenditure is that the environmental engineering department develops a general feasibility study of the various alternatives. On the basis of this study, one project is selected and analyzed in a very detailed manner in terms of the capital costs, operating costs and economic benefits, if they exist. Although the analysis is prepared by the environmental engineers, it is done with the assistance of the corporate engineering department, both centrally and in the field.

The primary pollution problem of the company is with the waste water from the pulp manufacturing process from which it is currently required to remove 85 percent of the dissolved and suspended solids. The company is planning to remove 95 percent of the solids in anticipation of more restrictive future requirements. The company uses an ammonium acid sulphite process for manufacturing the pulp and utilizes an incineration process for destroying the waste (dissolved solids) while recovering sulphur dioxide. This process is a good example of an integrated recycling process. The washing process in the pulp manufacturing produces waste which consists of 10 percent dissolved solids and 90 percent water. This solution then is evaporated until it is half dissolved solids, in which state it is burned as fuel in the manufacturing process. The burning gives off sulphur dioxide which is collected and converted into ammonium bisulphite and used as an input into the pulp process.

Measurement Activity

The capital costs of the environmental project include the costs of equipment which are identified specifically, on a very detailed level if necessary, as being part of the pollution control activity. The costs of the project engineers who work full-time on the project also are capitalized, but the costs of staff employees working part-time on the project are not determined directly, nor is any allocation procedure used. In addition, interest costs are capitalized, the rate being based on either the pollution control bond rate or the current market rate, depending on the method of financing used.

The operating costs of the pollution control equipment are isolated. The power costs are estimated from the total new power which is required to operate the equipment, less the value of the power savings generated by burning the residue (which could amount to the equivalent of 400,000 barrels of oil per year for a 600-ton per day mill). In addition, the operating costs are reduced by the value of the savings resulting from the recycling of the sulphur dioxide. Labor costs associated with operating the equipment also are isolated. It is interesting to note that the total of the power costs, labor costs and chemical savings results in net savings. However, the inclusion of maintenance costs and fixed costs (primarily interest, insurance and taxes) results in a net operating cost for the pollution control equipment. The engineers also undertook a sensitivity analysis to determine the effect of alternative oil prices on the economic prospects for the project.

The company also recognizes that it may have a savings resulting from the avoidance of legal penalties which would be imposed if it did not undertake the installation of pollution control equipment, but no attempt is made to quantify the savings because such an approach is not realistic in the modern business environment.

Company D—Non-Ferrous Metals

Organizational Structure and Environmental Problems

Company D is engaged in the mining, smelting and fabrication of non-ferrous metals.

The company is concerned primarily with two types of pollution—dusts and gasses—which are emitted as a result of its processing.

The company is decentralized, with a significant portion of the environmental control being the responsibility of the engineering area. Each plant has a plant engineer identified as having the localized pollution control responsibility. This person is in charge of knowing the current and planned pollution control laws and anticipating changes in these laws. He is responsible for identifying potential solutions to current company problems and preparing forecasts and tentative solutions for future problems.

Once a problem and potential solution have been identified at the plant level, the decision process moves to a more centralized base, where two groups serve in a staff capacity. One is the Environmental and Health Department, which includes an "environmental control group." This group interprets the laws and deals with the pollution control agencies. It also monitors ongoing pollution control and does sample testing on identified problems. The second group is the central Environmental Engineering Department, which is divided according to expertise in each of the environmental areas. This group is in charge of examining problem areas, developing alternative solutions for meeting current and anticipated laws, and preparing "rough" estimates of costs and timetables.

At this time an Environmental Review Committee examines the proposed project. This new committee must approve all significant pollution control expenditures. It is a high-level committee which includes production, medical, legal, environmental and engineering officers. Its function is defined broadly and includes examinations of differing, less expensive combinations of approaches, requests for extensions of time and/or variances, and potential legal proceedings. After an environmental expenditure is approved by this group, it is put into the regular evaluatory process for all capital expenditures.

Once an environmental capital project is approved, it goes back to Environmental Engineering where exact specifications, costs, and timetables are developed and implemented. A formal commitment is made to the pollution control agency, and construction is completed, tested, and goes on-line.

Measurement Activity

The company has developed a sophisticated computerized system for monitoring planned and actual capital costs of environmental projects. Once the projects become operational, however, the capital costs are subsumed into typical fixed-asset accounts. Environmental projects are defined as those which improve either the employee (internal) environment or the external environment. Environmental expenditures are defined as all those which are not required by the production system.

The environmental capital costs are limited primarily to out-of-pocket costs accumulated from the engineering specifications. Additional costs charged to the project would include any direct time put in by engineering personnel plus any employee costs incurred on the construction site. (These are limited to those employees whose jobs are full-time and would be eliminated when the project is completed.) It is estimated that up to 25 percent of new plant costs relate to pollution control expenditures. No allocation is made for legal, research and development, or environmental engineering costs, which are treated as operating costs.

Planned operating costs are limited primarily to increased maintenance costs and additional power costs. The power costs are becoming increasingly important because of the high consumption and short supply (quantity and quality) situation.

Benefits generally are not measured in monetary terms since, in most cases, the overriding concern is compliance with pollution control laws. In certain instances, reductions in various production costs are evaluated, and some proposed systems recoup valuable chemicals. When this is the case, these anticipated reduced chemical costs (offset by the costs of disposing of non-salable sludge) and savings in repairs, maintenance, and power of antiquated pollution control systems are offset against the increased operating costs. While this is not true in most cases, one such system enables the company to earn an acceptable return on its investment because the system has been refined to the point where it can be sold to competitors.

Some of these projects are financed by pollution control bonds, which may carry an interest rate as much as four percent lower than other debt financing. This financing is limited to equipment which causes virtually no improvement in productive capacity. Therefore, the company's information system is designed so these anticipated costs are coded separately from other environmental costs.

Company E—Food and Chemicals Manufacturing

Organizational Structure and Environmental Problems

Company E is a diversified manufacturing company with particular emphasis in the areas of food, consumer non-food, and specialty chemical operations. The corporate policy on environmental pollution is summarized by the following statement:

> Company E and its subsidiary companies must take an active part in the control of environmental pollution in all of its various forms. This obviously involves strict compliance with all pollution control laws, regulations and ordinances adopted by municipal, county, state, regional and federal pollution control agencies at all the locations of all its plants and operations. In addition to strict compliance with all regulations, it is the corporation's policy as a good corporate citizen to cooperate with civic, professional, industrial and research agencies in efforts to solve the problems of environmental pollution.

The company is organized on a very decentralized basis with approximately 16 divisions and about 130 separate legal entities. Each division has its own general manager and controller and is responsible for its own planning, budgeting, and profit and loss performance. Thus primary responsibility for pollution control rests with each division manager. However, the Engineering Policy Group, which has an energy engineer and a pollution engineer on its staff, has the responsibility of maintaining general surveillance over pollution control problems and of assisting operating management in developing engineering solutions to such problems.

Measurement Activity

Capital expenditure requests originate from the divisions. Requests of less than $75,000 may be approved within the division; those of less than $500,000 require approval from corporate management, while those over $500,000 require approval from the board of directors. The criteria for acceptance of a project are as follows: a growth project requires a higher return on investment before interest and taxes than does a cost savings project, while an essential project has no return requirement. Most pollution control expenditures fall into this latter category because they are necessary if the company is to remain in business.

The primary environmental problems faced by the company are air and water pollution. An example of an air pollution problem is a grain elevator which was allowing dust particles to escape into the atmosphere. This problem led to a particularly interesting decision because the need for the pollution control expenditures persuaded the company to evaluate whether to continue ownership of the elevator. The discounted future ongoing profits to be derived from the operation of the elevator less the current cost of complying with the pollution control laws exceeded the current sales price of the elevator, but the return was less than the cut-off required for the project. However, the investment was justified on non-quantitative grounds primarily because the elevator serves other divisions of the company, so better control of the quality of the supplies can be maintained. Other non-quantified benefits are improvements in employee efficiency, safety and health. An additional effect of the installation of the pollution control equipment is that it has approximately tripled the electricity consumption of the elevator. One interesting technical aspect of the problem is that there is no waste disposal problem because the dust collected as a ship is loaded has to be returned, by law, to that particular load.

An example of the company's water pollution problem involves the disposal of waste water effluent from processing plants. At one of its plants, the company is currently discharging the effluent into the river and is paying a waste treatment tax although no sewer is available to the factory. The company had the choice of building its own waste treatment plant or of using the municipal sewer system which is currently being planned. The company chose not to build its own plant even though it was expected to be the less expensive alternative. The company will pay an estimated half-million dollar assessment when it attaches to the sewer line but will treat it as an operating expense (special assessment) rather than as a capital investment.

The costs which are included in the capital costs of an environmental project are typical costs such as equipment, installation and engineering costs. Engineering costs can be included because all divisions are charged for engineering costs on an hourly rate. No research and development, interest, or legal costs are included, although the legal department must endorse all environmental projects. In the approval stage of the capital investment analysis, the company does not consider the tax effects of accelerated amortization or potential pollution control bond financing. These considerations are made after each project is approved. The company has not financed any environmental projects with pollution control bonds.

The company does not make any attempt to isolate pollution control capital costs for its internal reporting. Likewise no separate identification of the operating cost of pollution control equipment is made. Once in operation, these capital and operating costs are considered normal costs of doing business.

Company F—Tobacco

Organization Structure and Environmental Problems

Company F is a tobacco company, which is a division of a larger diversified management company. It has moderate external air and water pollution problems and also is concerned with internal environmental pollution.

Several years ago the top executives of the management company internalized pollution control as a major corporate objective. They issued a directive to each division that it was to go beyond the strictly legal requirements and meet "the intent of the law." It also created an environmental committee to coordinate environmental policy and to exert pressure upon operating division managers to consider the environmental impacts of decisions. Each operating division is now required to have an environmental coordinator and an environmental committee consisting of production, quality control, plant (environmental) engineering, research and development, and OSHA-related personnel. Company F's environmental engineer is responsible for knowing the details of compliance with federal and state pollution laws, for handling the contacts with these agencies, for energy consumption predictions, and for the coordination of engineering information related to pollution control bond requirements. This committee originally set up a program of work which involves identifying major projects, setting priorities, estimating the necessary appropriations, and setting up a timetable for completion. Initially, the committee was not concerned with cost effectiveness, but now it expects to become more formalized and sophisticated, with a corresponding increase in effectiveness surveillance.

Measurement Activity

In the planning stage of an environmental project, the environmental engineer determines the pollution control equipment necessary and goes to general contractors and consulting engineers to estimate total costs. No analysis is made of expected legal or research and development costs. Estimated operating costs are limited to electricity costs, maintenance costs and depreciation.

One particular environmental project involved the construction of a plant to recycle residual production from the other plants. Part of this plant was financed through the issuance of pollution control bonds. This required a careful analysis of construction costs, necessitating a close working liaison between the engineering and accounting departments. To determine the net capitalized cost subject to pollution control bond funding, the equipment costs were identified. These costs were limited to only that pollution control equipment which had no positive impact upon productivity. To this cost was added an allocated portion of the contractor's overhead (based on a pro rata share of direct costs multiplied by the total overhead) and an allocated portion of floor space (an opportunity cost based upon the square foot cost for each relevant portion of the building) where applicable. From these costs, the value of the recovered by-products was deducted. This value was calculated by multiplying the annual raw materials saved times a standard price, deducting taxes, and discounting these future cash savings over the life of the equipment at a market interest rate.

Actual environmental capital costs include those costs which current corporate policy requires to be capitalized. Detailed analysis is made of actual capitalized costs so that the company may take advantage of the investment credit and certain exemptions from state taxes. For actual ongoing operating costs, no effort is made to separate the operating costs of the pollution control equipment. The total standard cost of the pounds of recyclable material used is added back into operations as a raw material cost. Depreciation is kept separate in a subsidiary record but combined with all other depreciation costs for internal reporting.

Benefits of environmental expenditures are identified, although usually in a "checklist" fashion. Benefits associated with aesthetically pleasing landscaping and architecture include employee satisfaction, improved public image and reduced "housekeeping" costs. Before building a new plant, employees were queried concerning suggestions for improvements. These suggestions (which were incorporated into the design) included better lighting, more dust collection and air conditioning, "windowed" walls, and landscaping. It was noted that employees with more seniority opted for a new plant, resulting in lower absenteeism. As yet, no study has been initiated by the accounting or personnel departments to obtain post-investment information. Later, when a sufficient experience period has been achieved, such a study will be undertaken.

The company suggests that it goes beyond the current pollution control laws but does little to predict future laws. Two factors may account for this. First, air pollution control laws are based upon the weight of the particulate matter per pound of output. However, tobacco dust is so light that these laws are not particularly constraining. This enables the company to concentrate upon the economic feasibility of solving "housekeeping" problems. Second, the company is limited by external environmental equipment technology. Even though the company could "get by" by withdrawing 70 percent of the particulate matter, all current environmental equipment is designed to withdraw 97 percent.

Company G—Paper Products

Organizational Structure and Environmental Problems

Company G is a paper products company. Decisions regarding investments in environmental equipment involve three committees. The Finance Committee, which includes the president and vice-presidents of engineering, research and development, finance, and one of the major operating divisions, makes all the capital expenditure decisions. This committee is advised by the Executive Committee, which consists of the vice-presidents of the operating divisions, engineering, research and development, and finance. The third committee which affects decisions on environmental expenditures is the Research Policy Committee, which includes the chairman, president, the vice-president of engineering, research and development and two senior vice-presidents. This committee makes decisions regarding the direction of spending on research for the company, which will have a long-run impact on environmental expenditures. The director of environmental control, who reports to the vice-president of engineering, research and development, has the responsibility to see that the company is in compliance with legal requirements and to conduct negotiations with the various enforcement agencies. He is also the source of capital appropriation requests for environmental expenditures which are then submitted to the Finance Committee.

The major environmental problems faced by the company are air and water pollution, with water pollution currently being the more serious because the regulations are more restrictive. The effluent from the paper pulping process previously has been pumped into settling basins. However under current regulations this is not an acceptable pollution control method, so the company has designed and built its own patented chemical recovery process. The chemical recovery process consists of a drying process and the removal of chemicals which are then reused in the process or are sold to other companies. The residue is burned in the boilers. While this process is not considered to be economic, it does generate more than $800,000 total sales (including both internal and external) to offset the total costs of over $1,300,000 (on a full absorption basis) and is close to the break-even point on just the out-of-pocket costs. This recovery process does create its own pollution problem since it allows some chemical release into the atmosphere, and, of course, it does take energy to run the plant, Waste water is disposed of by spraying over an area of company-owned land.

The company is still experiencing the effects of its use of settling ponds five years ago. They are experiencing problems of seepage and are having to undertake a program of dredging the old ponds.

The air pollution problem faced by the company is primarily one of emissions from generating plants and is being solved by the installation of electrostatic precipitators.

Measurement Activity

Capital costs of environmental equipment include the costs of purchasing and constructing the facilities and the costs of engineering, which can easily be measured because the engineering department utilizes time cards. However, costs which are not included as capital costs are the development costs, consultants' fees, and interest. These costs are expensed as incurred.

The chemical recovery plant is treated as a separate cost center, within the profit center of pulp making, and its operating costs are treated accordingly. This is made practical primarily because of the separate physical nature of the chemical recovery plant. When costs are not readily separable, as with the electrostatic precipitators, the operating costs are not treated as a separate cost center but are included in the costs of power generation. The users of power are charged for the costs of generation, so the incremental pollution control costs are "lost" in the overall costs. It is interesting to note that power consumption has increased by 20 percent; 5 percent due to productive economic activity and 15 percent due to the addition of pollution control equipment.

Each environmental equipment investment alternative is separately analyzed to determine the desirability of using the pollution control facility accelerated amortization or the usual depreciation deduction for tax purposes.

The department of the director of environmental control is treated as a cost center within engineering, research and development but is not categorized separately as the costs are reported to higher levels of management.

In general the detailed records contain sufficient information to identify the cost associated with pollution control, but the company has not considered it desirable to categorize those items separately in reports which are prepared for management.

The company has not elected to utilize pollution control bonds for financing its investments. It has not considered them to be desirable because of the extra costs imposed by the additional reporting requirements and the complexities involved if the company decides to make changes in the characteristics of the investment subsequent to the acquisition of financing.

Company H—Non-Ferrous Metals

Organizational Structure and Environmental Problems

Company H is engaged in the mining and processing of non-ferrous metals and the manufacture of related products. The company is concerned presently with both air and water pollution as it attempts to meet existing pollution control standards. These pollution problems relate mainly to the refining of primary metals. Although not a current problem, it anticipates that the costs of solid waste disposal will become significant as such standards come on-line. It has spent over $100 million in pollution control equipment within the last three years and estimates that 30 percent of its capital expenditures are for that type of equipment.

Measurement Activity

Since the company is highly decentralized, it does not have a company-wide chart of accounts except for summary accounting figures reported to the main office. General accounting policy is set at corporate headquarters, but accounting practice is set at the division level. Each division has its own president, cost accountant and environmental expert.

The company prepares for each division a fairly complete Environmental Control Report for related capital expenditures, operating costs, indirect costs relating to environmental controls, and depreciation. The costs are accumulated for each major environmental impact (e.g., air and water) and are further categorized according to whether they affect the external or the internal environment. This report is prepared quarterly.

The company treats commercial environmental capital expenditures like any other capital expenditure. It capitalizes out-of-pocket engineering costs, all construction costs, interest based upon an overall corporate rate, and any "full-time" salaries of environmental project foremen. It identifies those expenditures which are necessary to implement adaptations to current operations separately from those necessary to replace existing facilities. These capital expenditures are classified into accounts such as dust and fume controls, water treatment facilities to control underground mine conditions, air conditioning, and noise control.

In one interesting situation, the company purchased an electric reverbatory furnace as a replacement for an existing furnace. The new furnace was more efficient but was also necessary to satisfy pollution control laws. The company considered the entire expenditure to be for pollution control because the old furnace had an indefinite life if properly maintained.

Current expenditures are classified in categories such as costs of operation, research, solid waste disposal, and the maintenance of restored land surfaces. Costs of operation would include out-of-pocket costs, primarily for labor and materials. Monitoring costs also would be included, but no measurement or allocation of power costs is made. Included in research would be all the costs associated with the division's environmental engineering department. Costs of solid waste disposal and maintenance of restored land surfaces are presently minor but potentially could be significant depending upon passage of solid waste pollution and strip-mining legislation.

Indirect costs relating to environmental controls include the costs of the centralized environmental engineering department, which services the production divisions, and miscellaneous expenditures.

Depreciation is computed separately for air pollution equipment and water pollution equipment. Under each section, the depreciation is further divided according to whether the equipment primarily affects the external or internal environment. These separate depreciation figures are presented only on the Environmental Control Report.

The company does not attempt to measure benefits because they generally are not economically significant to the company. The decision is made to select the "lowest cost" alternative which will meet current or predicted federal and state environmental regulations.

One of the methods used by the company to finance its environmental expenditures is via pollution control bonds, providing they fit into the total investment funding "picture."

Company I—Oil

Organizational Structure and Environmental Problems

Company I is an oil company which operates on a very decentralized basis. Corporate management sets policies and guidelines for operating departments and manages by exception rather than direction.

The environmental activities were handled entirely on a local level until about 10 years ago when a corporate coordinator was set up to advise, provide liaison, and interpret the various environmental policies of the company and government activities. The company has many diverse environmental problems but, as with other companies, air and water pollution are of the greatest current concern.

The following extracts from the budget manual summarize the company's approach to the measurement of environmental investments:

All capital investment proposals should include an assessment of the impact each project or program will have on the environment, recognizing that it may result in either a deterioration or an improvement in the quality of the environment.

The budget amounts should be further broken down into these economic categories:

a. *Meets Return Guidelines*—Projects which are considered (based on cost savings or market value increases) to meet established economic guidelines but which also would produce significant environmental conservation benefits.

b. *Necessary*—Projects which do not meet established economic guidelines but which are necessary to conform with existing or expected regulations and remain economically sound relative to other alternatives.

c. *Makes Some Contribution*—Projects which would contribute to the improvement of environmental quality but would not be required to conform to existing or expected regulations and which may show some economic benefit but fail to meet return guideline levels.

For investments which have both economic and environmental benefits, the American Petroleum Institute (API) has developed guidelines for determining the degree to which such investments should be categorized as environmental.[1] The company has developed its own guidelines which:

> correspond closely to current API guidelines. Identification of pollution abatement investments involves a considerable amount of subjective judgement, and it is anticipated that you will rely heavily on the present API report for guidance. The fundamental objective, however, is to obtain the most reasonable and practical estimates possible; and the individual circumstances involved should be considered in the application of the percentages.

For example, when a well is drilled, it is desirable to protect water sands surrounding the well from oil seepage by the installation of surface casing. However, a certain amount of casing is needed for the drilling of the well, and so the guidelines suggest that 50 percent of the cost of the surface casing should be considered environmental. The only person who can really determine the actual environmental percentage is the engineer on the site who can judge the amount of casing needed for the well as compared to the amount actually used. It is believed that some oil companies may use a considerably higher percentage of the cost of the surface casing as an environmental expenditure. This illustrates the difficulty of developing comparable figures.

Another interesting situation is the installation of a "CO" (carbon monoxide) boiler in a refinery. This was considered earlier an economic project where design conditions were not regulated, but it is classified now as 50 percent environmental when emission standards must be met.

An example of the difficult trade-offs involved in an environmental investment is provided by the decision to install wet gas scrubbers as opposed to electrostatic precipitators at the company's refineries. The wet gas scrubbers were the more expensive alternative, and they were expected to use more energy. In addition, they would take longer to get on-line which would require the company to obtain EPA and state agency concurrence to extend the compliance date. This action also would create the risk of citizens' suits against the company. However, they were chosen because there was a higher probability that they would meet current and future standards and be more reliable in operation as well as assist in the control of sulphur emissions.

Measurement Activity

The costs of environmental projects that are capitalized include the

---

[1] *Environmental Expenditures of the United States Petroleum Industry 1966-1973.* Publication No. 4233, American Petroleum Institute.

cost of the equipment and its installation, the costs of additional employees, and the costs of consultant engineers or lawyers. Excluded are the costs of the company's own engineering, legal or environmental staff and interest.

Separation of operating costs occurs only if the environmental unit is on a separate site. If not, the costs are charged against the particular operating unit. It is believed that separation could be achieved readily if it were considered desirable. The company does not separate depreciation expense on environmental assets.

For investments for which benefits are expected, the company estimates the benefits and includes them in any evaluation. However, it does not consider the opportunity cost of lost revenue, the avoidance of fine or the generation of employee benefits which may result. Little measurement of actual benefits occurs.

The company has used pollution control bonds for financing and has taken accelerated depreciation on Certified Pollution Control Facilities.

Summary and Conclusions

Some generalizations can be drawn from the case studies. Companies which are very active in the measurement of environmental impacts are so because of strong direction from top management. In the planning of environmental capital expenditures, engineers work very closely with the capital expenditure accounting personnel in the development of the systems and the related capital expenditure costs. These costs tend to be limited to equipment costs, with environmental engineering, research and development, and legal costs treated as expenses. In the case of expenditures which increase productivity and also abate pollution, there is a significant lack of agreement concerning allocation of the costs to these two functions. This appears to be due to the absence of standard definitions in the pollution control area. Very little measurement of benefits is made because companies view the possibility of shut-down as a critical, overriding benefit which eliminates the need for measuring any other benefits. Some companies attempt to evaluate benefits on a narrative basis. Environmental capital expenditures tend to be analyzed by the same methods as are used for traditional capital investments; however, accept/reject criteria are likely to be modified.

When environmental projects go on-line, the total costs generally do not continue to be categorized separately. Rather, they are subsumed within typical plant and equipment asset categories. Some companies take advantage of "pollution control" bond financing, but others feel that the paperwork and uncertainty involved more than offset any advantages.

Some companies separately categorize and measure ongoing pollution control operating costs, but these are generally in cases where a separate operating unit for that purpose can be identified. Other companies subsume operating costs in traditional cost categories but believe that they could measure environmental operating costs if it were necessary. No companies separately categorize depreciation on environmental assets for external reporting, and very few take advantage of Certified Pollution Control Facility accelerated amortization for tax purposes.

Most companies attempt to comply with current pollution control standards but build into their systems enough flexibility so that modifications can be made to comply with changes in such laws. Concern was expressed that only limited consideration is given by the various federal and state agencies to the economic feasibility of compliance with these laws, to the interaction between independently set water, air and land standards, and to the impact upon the consumption of scarce natural resources.

Chapter IV
Recommendations for Measurement and Decision Making Concerning Environmental Activity

This chapter is concerned with the integration of the information obtained from the questionnaire, the case studies, and a review of the relevant literature in order to develop a set of generalized recommendations regarding accounting and decision making pertaining to environmental activities.

The general nature of environmental costs is discussed in terms of definitions developed by various organizations. The categorization of environmental costs into initial, operating, and exit costs is developed. The nature of benefits, both internal and external, and their measurement are discussed. The chapter concludes with recommendations concerning the use of cost and benefit measurements for planning and control.

These recommendations should lead to the development of information rather than misinformation, enabling improved business decisions which, in turn, should lead to the fulfillment of corporate environmental objectives. It is hoped that these recommendations will be especially useful to companies which do not have extensive financial or personnel resources yet feel a social responsibility with respect to their environmental activities and wish to develop better information concerning such activities.

Environmental Cost Definition

The following definition of an environmental cost is proposed by the authors:

> An environmental cost is the incremental traceable cost which results from the activity of a company to improve the environment and to prevent, control, abate, or eliminate environmental deterioration. The cost includes expenditures to meet requirements promulgated by federal, state or local regulatory bodies, and expenditures incurred for voluntary corporation actions. If an

expenditure has a joint economic and environmental benefit, the environmental cost is that part of the expenditure which is incurred solely to produce environmental benefits.

The adoption of the above definition should lead to the reporting of information which is relatively comparable, reliable, and verifiable for both internal reporting and the reports required of the firm by such organizations as the EPA and SEC. Even though this definition was formulated subsequent to the case studies, it was not apparent from the discussion with the case study participants that the above definition would be unacceptable or unreasonable.

There are many possible ways in which to define environmental costs. However, two major problems stand out. First, to what extent should allocated costs be included in environmental costs? Second, when an expenditure is made which results in both environmental and economic benefits to the company, what portion of that expenditure should be considered an environmental cost?

Definitions of environmental costs have been developed by many organizations and varying approaches have been used in the resolution of these two problems. Some of these definitions are discussed in the following section.

Internal Revenue Service

The Internal Revenue Service has been concerned with the definition of the costs of pollution control facilities for two purposes. Companies may utilize tax exempt pollution control bonds for financing qualifying investments. Accelerated amortization also is available for Certified Pollution Control Facilities. The definitions are similar in both cases. For example, Regulation 1.103-8 (g) (2) of the Income Tax Regulations states that:

> If an expenditure for property would not be made but for the purpose of controlling pollution, and if the expenditure has no significant purpose other than the purpose of pollution control, the total expenditure for such property [qualifies as an expenditure for a pollution control facility] even though such property serves one or more functions in addition to its function as a pollution control facility.

In addition, the Regulation states that:

> an expenditure has a significant purpose other than the control of pollution if it results in an increase in production or capacity, or in a material extension of the useful life of a manufacturing or production facility or a part there . . . [in which case] only the incremental cost of such facility satisfies [the requirements of the law]. The 'incremental cost' of property is the excess of its total cost over that portion of its cost expended for a purpose other than the control of pollution.

The policy of the Internal Revenue Service concerning improvements built or paid for by companies is that the cost of the improvements not only includes payments made to outsiders in connection with the construction, but also the relevant part of the compensation of the company's regular employees and shareholders. In addition, the amount of overhead expenses incurred in connection with construction of buildings is included in the cost basis of the new building.

Thus the Internal Revenue Service approach is that the incremental total cost (including allocated overhead) should be considered as the cost of a pollution control facility. However, it may be difficult to determine the purpose of an expenditure and thus the amount of the incremental total costs that should be classified as environmental.

Council on Environmental Quality et al.

A joint publication by three governmental agencies uses the following definition:

> The investment costs of pollution control equipment were defined to include the direct incremental investment required to attain environmental standards ... The operating costs for pollution control equipment were defined to be incremental and net of any productivity increase or by-product revenues.[1]

Once again, from an accounting viewpoint the definition is not as clear as it could be. However, the use of the phrase "direct incremental" suggests that the allocated costs are to be excluded, and apparently the environmental portion of costs that have joint economic and environmental benefits are to be separated.

Department of Health, Education and Welfare

Another governmental report, *The Cost of Clean Air,* gives the following explanations of the phrase "cost of pollution control":

> Control costs are reported in terms of the initial investment required to establish control and the continuing annual expenses related to that investment. The investment cost is the total expense of purchasing and installing control equipment. The annual cost is the sum of yearly charges for capital-related costs (interest on the investment funds, property taxes where applicable, insurance premiums, and depreciation charges) plus operating (labor, utilities, and supplies) and maintenance costs.[2]

---

[1] "The Economic Impact of Pollution Control: A Summary of Recent Studies," Council on Environmental Quality, Department of Commerce, and the Environmental Protection Agency (Washington, D.C., March 1972), p. 7.

[2] The Second Report of the Secretary of Health, Education and Welfare, in compliance with PL 90-148, *The Clean Air Act,* as amended, March, 1970, in Seidler, Lee J. and Lynn L. Seidler, *Social Accounting* (Los Angeles: Mellville Publishing Company, 1975), p. 284.

This report also is vague about what is included in the initial cost but probably would include allocated overhead costs. The report does not address the problem of investments which have a joint economic and environmental benefit. The definition of annual costs is unusual since it includes the interest on the funds invested, in addition to depreciation.

The Conference Board

In the development of national cost data for water pollution abatement facilities, The Conference Board[3] did not define costs but merely asked the respondents to "estimate the capital expenditures for the purpose of water pollution abatement" at each plant. However, it did specify that the report should include ". . . only those expenditures made for the purpose of pollution abatement. If improvements have been made in the production process which provide an incidental benefit in the abatement of pollution, *do not* include the expenditure for that improvement." Similarly, respondents were asked to report "annual expenditures for operating and maintaining existing water pollution facilities" without specifically defining which particular costs should be included.

Thus, this report takes a very restrictive view of environmental investment since any investment which has an economic benefit is excluded in contrast to most of the other definitions. It also fails to specify whether allocated costs should be included.

The American Petroleum Institute

The American Petroleum Institute (API) has developed guidelines which are used by oil companies to respond to a periodic questionnaire regarding their environmental expenditures.[4] Its definition is as follows:

> Environmental Protection Expenditures are considered to be all those expenditures related to the prevention, control, abatement or elimination of environmental pollution. They include, but are not limited to expenditures which meet definitions promulgated by federal, state, or local regulatory bodies or those which meet tax relief provisions. The questionnaire includes three categories of such expenditures: air, water, and land and other. The latter includes expenditures for such items as solid waste management, noise abatement, and beautification.

---

[3] Leonard Lund, *Industry Expenditures for Water Pollution Abatement* (New York, The Conference Board, Inc., 1972), pp. 58-61.

[4] *Environmental Expenditures of the United States Petroleum Industry 1966-1973, op. cit.*

Furthermore, it states that:

> Many expenditures cannot be attributed entirely to "environmental protection." In all such cases, appropriate consideration should be given to motivation: What were the principal factors involved in the expenditure decision? How large a role did considerations of environmental protection play in that decision?
>
> Reported costs should not include the loss of revenue or estimates of business "loss" as a result of conditions associated with environmental protection. The speculative nature of such cost items and the difficulty of justifying methods used to develop them could be construed as unrealistic reporting designed to make the industry's total expenditures for environmental protection appear larger than they actually were.
>
> In some instances estimates of environmental protection expenditures must be based on incremental concepts and will be heavily dependent on engineering judgment. For example, if a unit meets good business operating requirements under normal design concepts, but requires modifications or additions because of environmental considerations, then the estimated cost of modifications or additions logically should be attributed to environmental protection . . . Investments which yield acceptable rates of return logically may be included as environmental expenditures if, in fact, they meet the above-mentioned criteria.

The API questionnaire then lists 175 types of capital expenditures and the suggested percentage of each that should be considered to be environmental. The instructions state that the companies should

> use the suggested percentage of total cost when you allocate expenditures to environmental protection . . . In all cases include increased incremental costs resulting from environmental considerations.

The above instructions are somewhat confusing because they do not make clear whether only incremental costs should be reported, or whether some percentage of total project costs should be reported, and, if the latter, how the percentage should be determined. It appears that it is the intention of the API to use the latter approach, although the criteria that a company should use to develop a percentage other than the recommended one is not clear.

Similar problems exist with the reporting of periodic expenses. The API questionnaire states that

> When your company records identify current expenses applicable to environmental protection activities, report such expenses by a function as incurred. Report maintenance, operating and administrative expenses by function as available from accounting records. Do not include depreciation . . .

When environmental protection expenses for administration and operations and maintenance must be estimated, it is recommended that the total expenses be allocated according to the proportion of the gross capital investment which is for environmental facilities.

Thus the API is recommending that a company should use actual costs, if available, no matter what criteria have been used in their accumulation. Furthermore, it suggests that administrative expenses be allocated to the environmental expenses. However, this may mislead readers because administrative expenses normally are reported as a line item in the income statement rather than being allocated to functions.

The above criticisms illustrate the difficulties of developing criteria which will lead to reliable and comparable reporting even by companies in a single industry. The API should be commended for its efforts to report environmental expenditures, particularly for its developoment of the suggested percentages to be used for investments which have joint economic and environmental benefits. It would be beneficial if other industries developed the same kind of procedures, particularly if all the groups reported their expenditures on the basis of the recommendations made in this monograph.

Definition of Environmental Cost

The main criticism of the above selected definitions of environmental costs is that they are not sufficiently specific with regard to what is to be included in and excluded from an environmental cost. The result of imprecise definitions will be that the numbers collected from various sources under each particular definition will not necessarily be comparable. Since the definitions vary among sources, the total numbers accumulated under the various definitions will not be comparable.

The above definitions and related discussion indicate that there basically are four possible definitions of an environmental cost:

(1) the incremental traceable cost incurred for the environmental aspects of a project

(2) the total cost incurred for the environmental aspects of a project

(3) the incremental traceable cost incurred for the total project for which the primary motivation is to produce environmental benefits

(4) the total cost incurred for the total project for which the primary motivation is to produce environmental benefits.

Alternatives (1) and (3) do not include allocated costs and (3) and (4) do not distinguish that part of the total cost which is incurred to produce environmental benefits from that part which produces economic benefits.

Alternative (1) produces the lowest environmental cost, whereas (4) produces the highest cost.

The results of the questionnaire and the case studies did not indicate that any single definition is currently in widespread use. Therefore, the authors feel that the best approach is to develop the most satisfactory conceptual definition. It is to be hoped that a uniform definition may enjoy widespread adoption and thus reduce the confusion that currently exists.

It is the opinion of the authors that neither (3) nor (4) is satisfactory because each involves a subjective and perhaps arbitrary approach. What criteria are used to determine the primary motivation? Who applies the criteria to a particular expenditure? What if the primary motivation is for environmental reasons, but the primary benefit is economic? Because of such questions, it is undesirable to consider an environmental cost as being the total cost (whether incremental or not) incurred because a company undertakes an activity for which the primary motivation is the development of environmental benefits.

Alternatives (1) and (2) require that the costs incurred to produce environmental benefits be isolated from those incurred to produce economic benefits.

In those situations in which the environmental investment consists of a physical addition to the company's existing assets (for example, adding fans, ducts, and bag houses to remove particulate emissions from a furnace), and the investment has no direct economic benefit to the company, then the measurement is relatively simple. All the incremental costs of the investment reasonably can be considered to be environmental.

A much more significant problem exists when the environmental aspects of an asset are not physically separate from the economic aspects as, for example, when a new asset is acquired in which environmental controls are built in. What part of the cost is for the environmental control, and what part is for the economically productive asset itself? If a similar asset having no environmental controls included is available, the difference between the costs of the two assets reasonably should be considered to be the cost of the environmental controls. However, it is not likely that such an asset would be available because as the need for environmental controls becomes institutionalized worldwide, some types of equipment are no longer manufactured without built-in environmental controls. The measurement problems will have to be solved by an analysis (on a very detailed basis, if necessary) of the use to which each component of the asset is put—environmental control or productive activity. Discussions with the engineers of the companies which participated in this research project indicated that such classification is possible on a reliable basis. Some individual components may serve both the environmental and economic aspects, but no situation was noted in which the cost of such components would be material. As a last resort, if classification becomes impossible, a simple arbitrary allocation could be used for that component. Initially, a classification of the costs of each component of those assets which have built-in environmental controls would take some time and effort, but this would become minimal as such classification becomes routine.

The authors believe that alternative (1) is more desirable than alternative (2). Thus, environmental costs should include only incremental traceable costs and should exclude allocated costs, such as general and administrative overhead. Since overhead classifications and methods of allocation vary among and within firms, a significant degree of standardization would be lost if overhead allocations were included. Furthermore, a primary purpose of business is to provide products desired by society while making a reasonable profit, and the prevention of pollution is an ancillary requirement. Therefore, environmental cost should include only the incremental costs and not an allocated portion of the costs incurred by the company to facilitate its normal economic activity. Thus the authors suggest the definition as proposed on pages 47 and 48.

Environmental Cost Categories

Costs associated with environmental activities may be categorized into three groups: initial costs, which are incurred in order to get the activity on-line; operating costs, which are recognized while the activity is operating; and exit costs, which are incurred to close down the activity. It can be seen that some of the suggested cost categories are different from those utilized in the questionnaire and reported in Chapter II. These changes were made because of the results obtained from the questionnaire and from the discussions held with the case study companies.

Initial Costs

Many types of costs are incurred before an environmental project becomes operational. Policy with regard to whether or not these costs should be capitalized or expensed should follow accepted standards of financial reporting and is not a concern of this study.

It is suggested that initial costs be categorized as follows: land costs, equipment costs, engineering costs, research and development costs, and miscellaneous costs.

Land costs include all the incremental traceable costs of land that is utilized for pollution abatement. This includes land that is used for buildings and equipment as well as land used for settling ponds or the disposal of waste. Any aesthetic improvements to land owned by a company also should be included. However a clear distinction needs to be drawn between routine beautification of land surrounding an office building and aesthetic improvement of land undertaken for environmental reasons.

Equipment costs include all the incremental traceable costs incurred for pollution abatement equipment, including machinery and buildings, and their transportation, installation, and testing.

Engineering costs associated with environmental investments should be categorized separately. Some companies have engineering departments devoted solely to environmental matters, in which cases the total traceable costs of these departments should be categorized as environmental engineering costs. When the environmental engineers are part of a total engineering department, then the costs of those people working full-time or part-time on environmental activities should be categorized separately. The costs of certain support personnel and some overhead costs may also be incremental costs but should not be included on the basis of an arbitrary allocation procedure.

Research and development costs for environmental activities should be identified and categorized on the same basis as the engineering costs.

Miscellaneous costs include such items as the legal costs (and possible payment of fines) and image promotion costs, in the form of advertising or employee time, which are related to the planning and development of the company's environmental activities.

The above areas are the primary categories that should be used for identifying the initial environmental cost. However variations in the categorization may be appropriate. For example, in many smaller firms, the engineering and research and development departments may be combined into one department. In these cases an attempt to identify separate categories would not be beneficial. If a company became involved in significant litigation, it might be appropriate to identify separately the legal costs as they become material.

Operating Costs

Once a company has installed pollution abatement equipment, it will incur certain operating costs associated with that equipment. These operating costs can be classified as follows: equipment operating costs, additional production costs, maintenance costs, disposal costs, monitoring costs, depreciation, and miscellaneous costs.

Operating costs of pollution control equipment including labor, materials, and any incremental overhead should be categorized separately. Typically, the identification of the cost of labor and direct materials used for the operation of pollution control equipment should not present major difficulties. However, the identification of other incremental costs may be more problematic. For example, much pollution control equipment uses a considerable amount of energy. If the energy comes from an outside source (e.g., electricity supplied by a utility company), the addition of some form of metering unit should enable specific identification of these costs. In some situations in which power is generated internally and not supplied in a form that can be metered readily, difficulties in measuring actual costs may arise. However, from discussions with the participating companies, it appears that reliable and accurate estimates can be made in the majority of situations where direct measurement is not possible.

The installation of pollution control equipment also may adversely affect the costs of producing the products of the firm. For example, it may lead to a change to the use of more expensive materials or to the use of a less efficient or a more labor intensive production process. The estimation of these costs is desirable in the planning stage, but the measurement of the actual period of incremental production costs may present considerable pragmatic measurement problems.

The incremental traceable costs incurred for the maintenance of the pollution control equipment, primarily labor and materials, should be readily identifiable for a company which has a reasonably sophisticated accounting system.

Disposal costs are the incremental traceable costs incurred that are associated with the adequate disposal of waste products which are not recycled. These waste products may be from either the pollution control equipment (e.g., the particulate matter collected in bag houses) or directly from the production process if no pollution control equipment is utilized.

Monitoring costs are the incremental traceable costs of labor, supplies and perhaps overhead incurred to monitor the compliance with predetermined acceptable levels of pollution. These may be costs associated with continuous monitoring, such as the control of emissions from blast furnaces, or periodic monitoring, such as the checking of ambient air quality at sites surrounding a factory.

Since some of the initial costs of pollution control equipment will be capitalized, depreciation expense will be charged. Normal financial accounting rules should be followed to determine the method of depreciation and hence the amount of the depreciation in any particular period. For planning purposes, the company should recognize the tax savings which result from the additional depreciation. If the facility qualifies for accelerated amortization allowed for Certified Pollution Control Facilities, then the tax savings may be correspondingly larger.[5] It should be recognized

---

[5] Although Congress instituted the Certified Pollution Control Facility accelerated amortization in order to stimulate pollution control investment, this amortization may not always be a desirable tax deduction for a company. Depending upon the estimated life of the equipment, the company's marginal tax rate, and the company's cost of capital, it may be found that the company will maximize the present value of its tax savings by electing to take the usual depreciation deduction and investment credit instead of the accelerated amortization. For a more complete discussion, see Loren A. Nikolai and Donald E. Ricketts, "The Use of 'Certified Pollution Control Facility' Amortization: An Optimal Strategy?" *Volume II: Contributed Sessions Papers, Fifth Annual Midwest AIDS Conference* May 10-11, 1974), p. T37.

that for all the expenses of pollution control equipment, the true cost to the company is the total expenses net of the tax savings which accrue to the company. Miscellaneous costs include such items as the company's ongoing legal and image promotion costs.

Exit Costs

The final category of costs associated with pollution control equipment is the incremental traceable costs incurred by a company when it exits from an investment. These will be primarily restoration costs in which land is restored to approximately its original condition. For example, in strip mining operations, these costs may be very significant.

Environmental Cost Scorecard

It may be possible that the determination of each of the environmental costs may not reflect adequately all of the characteristics of the project. For example, a company may be able to measure accurately the costs of disposing of its waste products. However, it may also recognize (although not monetarily) that the disposal will create public relations problems even though the company is satisfying all environmental requirements. The experience of one of the companies in a case study provides a second example. The company had agreed with the relevant environmental authorities to monitor pollution from its factory by building towers with monitoring equipment at various points around the factory. These were to be placed on land owned by company employees. The company could determine the costs and had the agreement of the required employees. However, objections were raised by members of the community against the erection of the towers, and these objections placed the whole program in jeopardy. These examples illustrate that it may be necessary to provide a measurement system with the flexibility to include non-quantifiable factors associated with the costs.

Exhibit 15 is an "environmental cost scorecard" which includes not only a column for the amounts associated with each cost but also a section for a statement of the descriptive considerations associated with each cost category. The scorecard can be used to accumulate the costs for a particular project or projects, or it can be used to accumulate the costs accruing (on a planned or actual basis) during a particular period.

Environmental Benefits

In the initial consideration of the benefits which might arise as a result of environmental expenditures, a company may recognize the primary benefit from such investments to be the ability to remain in business and avoid legal costs and fines. This benefit may be perceived to be of such overriding magnitude that it negates the necessity of measuring any other benefits. While this is a significant benefit, the measurement of other benefits is important for four reasons. First, a company may face a choice of either making an environmental expenditure to be in compliance with a current pollution control standard or of making such an expenditure in

EXHIBIT 15

ENVIRONMENTAL COST SCORECARD

	Amount	Descriptive Considerations

Initial Costs
  1. Land
  2. Equipment
  3. Engineering
  4. Research & Development
  5. Miscellaneous		

Operating Costs
  1. Equipment Operating
  2. Additional Production
  3. Maintenance
  4. Disposal
  5. Monitoring
  6. Depreciation
  7. Miscellaneous		

Exit Costs		

order to comply with a perceived future pollution control standard (or simply a self-imposed standard in excess of the current requirements). The measurement of all the benefits would enable management to compare the attractiveness of the two alternatives. Second, as more technologies become available, a company may have two or more ways of solving its environmental problem. Measurements of benefits would be useful in evaluating the total impact of each alternative. Third, the identification and measurement of environmental benefits will impart a more positive, favorable image upon such projects. Division managers may view such expenditures with less pessimism if these projects are viewed as more than just "additional cost" expenditures. Finally, on an ongoing basis, a company will be able to better assess its success in the achievement of its social responsibility goals by comparing the actual benefits attained with the planned benefits.

In order to accumulate complete environmental information, it is necessary to define an environmental benefit. An environmental benefit is defined as follows:

> An environmental benefit is a benefit to the environment which results from an expenditure of an environmental cost.

The environmental benefit must be distinguished from an economic benefit if both result from a single expenditure. Benefits may be categorized further as internal and external as follows:

> Internal environmental benefits are those environmental benefits which directly benefit the company while indirectly benefiting society.

> External environmental benefits are those environmental benefits which directly benefit society while indirectly benefiting the company.

It is important that a company identify and measure both sets of benefits. However, certain measurement adjustments are necessary. In traditional economic analysis, benefits which accrue to the company usually are described as either reductions in costs or increases in revenues, both of which require monetary measurements. However, it may not be possible to determine the precise monetary impacts of environmental benefits. Therefore, while the measurement of monetary impacts should be the ultimate goal, identification of benefits and a descriptive indication of their direction and magnitude may be the most feasible approach. With this in mind, the use of a "benefits scorecard," as illustrated in Exhibit 16, is suggested. On this scorecard, both internal and external benefits are identified along the left-hand side, while a column is provided for three types of measurements: monetary, quantitative but non-monetary, and non-quantitative. Where non-quantitative measurements are necessary, the authors suggest the use of the descriptive categories: (1) "significant," representing a likely significant impact on reduced costs or increased revenues or externalities; (2) "moderate," representing a likely moderate impact; or (3) "slight," representing some, but limited impact. In certain situations it may be possible to develop more precise ratings.

Admittedly this evaluation procedure is imprecise, but it does enable the company to accumulate on a single source document a summary of all the benefits derived from all of its environmental activities. Thus, the benefits scorecard can be used to accumulate benefits for a particular project or projects, or it can be used to accumulate the benefits accruing (on a planned or actual basis) during a particular time period. Each of these sets of benefits is discussed below. Although all of these benefits may not be applicable to each company in each industry, every company should identify those benefits which apply in its situation.

EXHIBIT 16

ENVIRONMENTAL BENEFITS SCORECARD

Benefit	Monetary	Measurement Quantitative (Non-Monetary)	Non-Quantitative (Descriptive)

Internal:

1. Recyclable raw materials
2. Energy production
3. By-product sales
4. Development of saleable processes
5. Improved working conditions:
   a. reduced turnover
   b. ability to attract new employees
   c. reduced absenteeism
   d. improved employee efficiency
6. Improved "good citizenship" reputation

External (water): Improvements in

1. Public water supply
2. Swimming & other sports
3. Fish & wildlife support
4. Agricultural & industrial water supply
5. Navigation
6. Health
7. Aesthetics
8. Overall impact

External (air): Improvements in

1. Health
2. Agricultural vegetation
3. Wild vegetation
4. Property damage
5. Wildlife support
6. Aesthetics
7. Overall impact

Internal Environmental Benefits

As defined above, internal environmental benefits are those which directly benefit the company while indirectly benefiting society. The discussion of particular benefits will proceed from the more obvious measurable benefits to the less obvious ones.

(1) Recyclable raw materials

Certain pollution abatement processes enable the company to recover valuable raw materials, such as chemicals, which can be recycled into the productive process. This recycling becomes even more important when it concerns raw materials which are in short supply and whose temporary absence may affect the quality and quantity of the production output. Reused raw materials represent a cost savings which can be measured in monetary terms. Such measurement requires an identification of the type and quantity of material to be recycled, along with the unit cost which would be paid if purchased externally. This unit cost should include the anticipated future purchase price (considering possible shortages), as well as applicable handling and freight charges. The units saved multiplied times the external unit cost represents the savings due to recycling.

(2) Energy production

The company may be able to utilize as fuel the by-product from the pollution abatement process. Some companies have had to curtail production because of inadequate fuel supplies. In addition, because of this fuel shortage, much higher fuel costs are being incurred. The burning of pollution abatement by-products may be economically advantageous and at the same time conserve scarce natural resources. An estimation of the cost savings will entail multiplying the amount of energy which is generated from each unit of by-product times the external purchase price.

(3) By-product sales

Certain products resulting from pollution abatement, while not useable to the company, may be useable by other companies. Whether salable directly to these companies or through an intermediary, the total revenues from these by-product sales should be determined.

(4) Development of salable processes

In addition to the sale of by-products, it is possible that the company may develop its own pollution abatement process. Such a process may include new types of machinery or only a method of combining more efficiently the existing technology. In either case, consideration should be given to the measurement of the profits which are likely to accrue from these sales. Where monetary information is not available, a descriptive evaluation should be utilized.

(5) Improved working conditions

An improvement in working conditions benefits the company in several ways. These include reduced turnover, the ability to attract new employees, reduced absenteeism, and improved employee efficiency. Each of these can result in the reduction of costs.

a) *reduced turnover*—higher attrition of employees causes correspondingly higher hiring and training costs. Some of this attrition may be due to the pollution created by the productive process. A reduction in such pollution may tend to reduce attrition, thereby reducing hiring and training costs. It is difficult, however, to isolate such a cause of changing recruitment costs from other contributing factors. Therefore, it is suggested that reduced turnover be evaluated descriptively in the short run with "before" and "after" quantitative turnover information accumulated in the longer run.

b) *ability to attract new employees*—more attractive working and living conditions brought about by pollution control are likely to attract a larger potential work force to the locality in general and to the company specifically. A job search process which is initiated by the prospective employee reduces the search costs on the part of the company. These reduced costs should be included as a benefit of an environmental activity. Once again, these benefits are difficult to measure monetarily, and, therefore, the use of a descriptive evaluation is suggested.

c) *reduced absenteeism*—absenteeism, whether caused by poor health or a desire to avoid pollutive substances, results in a lack of productivity. The reduction of such absenteeism through pollution abatement is likely to increase production correspondingly, thereby reducing costs on a per unit basis. In the short run, this benefit should be evaluated descriptively. In the longer run, quantitative personnel information can be accumulated concerning the absenteeism within a certain portion of the plant with respect to an environmental activity.

d) *improved employee efficiency*—pollution abatement expenditures may cause improved employee efficiency by, for example, improving visual conditions or reducing the number of necessary "breaks." Such improvements reduce unit costs, and, if feasible, should be measured separately. Again, the state of the art does not enable quantitative measurements, and a descriptive evaluation is suggested.

(6) Public acceptance

Most companies are concerned with their image as a "good citizen" in the locality within which they operate. Such a reputation benefits the company in numerous, immeasurable ways including favorable disposition toward the company concerning the levying of taxes, the availability of a pool of potential employees, and the provision of municipal services. Certain pollution abatement alternatives, more so than others, may enhance the company's "good citizen" reputation and should be identified on a descriptive basis on the scorecard.

In addition to the above savings, any reductions in costs such as the avoidance of any temporary "down time" costs should be included in the internal environmental benefits.

External Environmental Benefits

External environmental benefits are defined as those that directly benefit society while indirectly benefiting the company as a member of society. Although the relationship may be indirect, it is useful to identify and measure such benefits. External benefits may be classfied in a number of different ways. One scheme identifies four broad beneficial areas: health, production, aesthetics and ecology.[6] Health includes all human health-related impacts on an environmental project. Production includes usages associated with all industrial, municipal and domestic facilities. Aesthetics includes all aesthetic considerations directly or indirectly related to the environment. Finally, ecological considerations include all direct or indirect impacts upon ecosystems. Although these have been developed with respect to water quality, they seem to be applicable to other environmental areas as well. While these are useful categories for an initial classification, benefits need to be more specifically identified to be of assistance in this analysis.

Most current measurements of air, water and land pollution are expressed in biological, chemical or other physical science terminology. Unfortunately, these expressions may not be readily understandable to many individuals, and different segments of society may be able to tolerate differing degrees of pollution. Some way of expressing such differences is desirable.

What is needed is a single, easy to understand measurement unit which could be used to express the impact of a particular pollution abatement project upon the various polluting substances and their relative im-

---

[6] D. L. Jordening and James K. Allwood, *Research Needs and Priorities: Water Pollution Control Benefits and Costs,* Volume II, U.S. Environmental Protection Agency (Washington: Government Printing Office, 1973), p. 63.

pact upon the specific users, as is illustrated in the following diagram:

Geographic Area

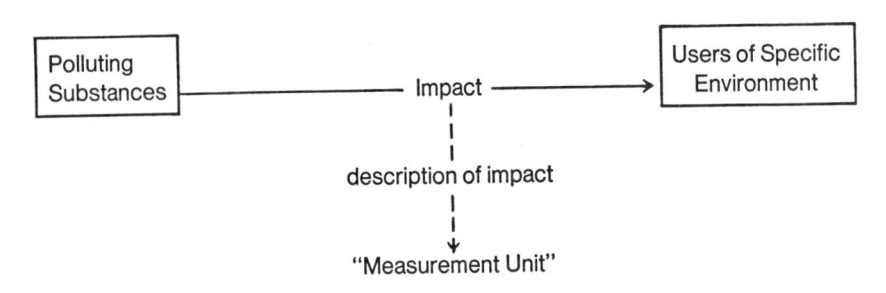

```
┌──────────┐                              ┌──────────────┐
│ Polluting│                              │Users of Specific│
│Substances│─────────── Impact ──────────▶│ Environment  │
└──────────┘                              └──────────────┘
                            │
                            │
                  description of impact
                            │
                            ▼
                   "Measurement Unit"
```

The development of this measurement unit entails a four-step process: (1) specification of the geographic area, (2) identification of the polluting substances, (3) identification of the users (and their needs) of the specific environment, and (4) an expression of the relationship between these variables in the form of a measurement unit. If the project involved air pollution, then air polluting substances and differing types of air users within a specified geographic region would need to be identified and the relationships measured and reported. A similar analysis would be undertaken concerning water pollution abatement. While this is relatively easy to conceptualize, it is exceedingly difficult to implement.

Several initial thrusts have been made into the development of a model to produce some form of measurement unit for environmental benefits. These models have dealt primarily with water pollution. Each has attempted to measure water quality, which has been interpreted as referring to physical or aesthetic properties or a composite of the two. Several water quality characteristics are listed in Exhibit 17. Two particularly interesting models concerning such measurements are discussed in an Environmental Protection Agency publication.[7] The first is by Pratt, Parranello, and Pesarin who have developed a classification system for ranking water quality with an index number ranging from 1 to 8. However, this system is based solely upon physical characteristics and does not consider differing geographic locations.

The second, developed by Battelle's Columbus Laboratories involves a complex environmental evaluation system for water resource planning. This system ranks composite environmental quality on a "parameter importance units" scale from 0 to 1,000. Components include ecology (subdivided into species and population, habitats, communities, and ecosystems), environmental pollution (subdivided into land, air, water, biota,

---

[7]*Ibid.*, p. 86.

EXHIBIT 17

SELECTED WATER QUALITY CHARACTERISTICS

Physical Characteristics

Biochemical oxygen demand (BOD)
Dissolved oxygen (DO)
Chemical oxygen demand (COD)
Fecal coliform bacteria
Total dissolved solids (TDS)
Total suspended solids (TSS)
Hydrogen-ion concentration (pH)
Inorganic phosphate
Inorganic nitrogen
Inorganic carbon
Temperature
Hardness (as $CaCO_3$)
Specific electric conductance
Radioactivity
Toxic substances (including pesticides)
Turbidity
Color
Oil

Aesthetic Characteristics

Taste
Appearance
Odor
Floating materials
Shoreline appearance
Biota
Man-made objects
Human interest

Source: D. L. Jordening and James K. Allwood, *Research Needs and Priorities: Water Pollution Control Benefits and Costs,* Volume II, U. S. Environmental Protection Agency (Washington: Government Printing Office, 1973) p. 87.

man-made objects, and composition) and human interests (including educational/scientific packages, historical packages, cultures, mood/atmosphere, and life patterns).

Dinius has developed another measurement model for use in evaluating the impacts of water pollution.[8] A single measurement called a "quality unit" is used to express the degree of pollution in the water as a percentage of "perfect" water. This overall quality unit is a composite of the individual quality units for each pollution category weighted by the importance of each category to the overall pollution level.

Four polluting categories are identified. These include the (1) quantity of organic materials present, (2) quantity of coliform bacteria present, (3) quantity of ionic matter present, and (4) physical characteristics. Eleven standard types of water analyses are used to identify the amount of pollution in these categories.

Six different water uses are identified so that all preferences can be considered in the development of the importance weightings. These uses include (1) public water supply, (2) swimming and other water contact sports, (3) fish, shellfish, and wildlife support, (4) agricultural and industrial water supply, (5) navigation, and (6) treated waste transportation.

The development of the overall quality unit consists of four steps. First, a general rating scale is created to establish the standard, according to classes of users, to be used in developing separate rating sacles for the results of each type of water analysis. An example of the general rating scale for the quality unit is shown in Exhibit 18.

Next an individual rating scale for each analysis is developed so that the correlation between the results of each analysis and its contribution to water pollution can be determined. Third, equations for each individual test are formulated in order to convert raw data into individual quality units. Finally, because certain tests were deemed to be more significant than others to water quality, the individual quality units in the third step are weighted for importance. The final result is a weighted formula for calculating the overall quality of the water at one point in time.

Although the general rating scales, the individual scales, and the weights are somewhat subjective, the overall technique is not. With refinement, this reporting system may prove to be an extremely useful and understandable tool.

This same type of quality unit could be established for air pollution. Ratings of air pollution categories such as carbon monoxide, sulphur oxides, nitrogen oxides, and particulate matter could be developed and related to user groups so that an air quality unit could be determined. The U.S. Department of Health, Education, and Welfare has developed fig-

---

[8]S.H. Dinius, "Social Accounting System for Evaluating Water Resources," *Water Resources Research,* Volume 8, No. 5 (October 1972), pp. 1159-1177.

EXHIBIT 18

GENERAL RATING SCALE FOR THE QUALITY UNIT

PERCENT OF PURE WATER	Public Water Supply	Recreation	Fish Shellfish and Wildlife	Industrial and Agricultural	Navigation	Treated Waste Transportation
100	PURIFICATION NOT NECESSARY	ACCEPTABLE FOR ALL WATER SPORTS	ACCEPTABLE FOR ALL FISH	PURIFICATION NOT NECESSARY	ACCEPTABLE	ACCEPTABLE
90	MINOR PURIFICATION REQUIRED			MINOR PURIFICATION NECESSARY FOR INDUSTRY REQUIRING QUALITY WATER		
80	NECESSARY TREATMENT					
70	BECOMING MORE EXTENSIVE	BECOMING POLLUTED — STILL ACCEPTABLE BACTERIA COUNT	MARGINAL FOR TROUT	NO TREATMENT NECESSARY FOR NORMAL INDUSTRY		
60			DOUBTFUL FOR SENSITIVE FISH			
50	DOUBTFUL	DOUBTFUL FOR WATER CONTACT	HARDY FISH ONLY	EXTENSIVE TREATMENT FOR MOST INDUSTRY		
40		ONLY BOATING NO WATER CONTACT	COARSE FISH ONLY			
30	NOT ACCEPTABLE	OBVIOUS POLLUTION APPEARING	NOT ACCEPTABLE	ROUGH INDUSTRY USE ONLY	OBVIOUS POLLUTION APPEARING	
20		OBVIOUS POLLUTION — NOT ACCEPTABLE		NOT ACCEPTABLE	OBVIOUS POLLUTION — NOT ACCEPTABLE	
10						NOT ACCEPTABLE
0						

Source: S. H. Dinius, "Social Accounting System for Evaluating Water Resources," *Water Resources Research*, Vol. 8, No. 5 (October, 1972), p. 1163.

ures for damages to health, materials, property values, and vegetation for each type of air pollution.[9] However, these have been developed on a macro basis and may not be useful for individual companies. In addition, the National Wildlife Federation develops its annual indices of Environmental Quality relating to soil, timber, living space, wildlife, minerals, water, and air.[10] They are also on a macro basis but may provide the reader with some helpful classification schemes.

While the use of a specific model is not necessarily advocated, it is suggested that, through a combination of the above, the reduction in the quantities of polluting substances and each group of users or uses be identified and ranked in importance. Finally, some sort of common measurement unit should be established and the relative impacts upon these users or uses identified on the scorecard.

Planning

The planning of pollution abatement originates with the development of organizational policies and the establishment of an organizational structure.

The case study companies exhibited differing approaches to the problems of organizing for environmental planning. Companies that are most active in environmental measurements appear to internalize pollution abatement as a top management objective and have set forth this objective in the form of company policy. This policy should state that the company will adhere to all existing pollution control laws, will attempt to anticipate future pollution control laws, and will consider its "good citizenship" obligations of going beyond such laws in its efforts to assure a healthy and satisfying physical environment. It is suggested that such a policy be implemented by each concerned company and that by setting the policy at the highest level, internal direction can be given to lower-level managers. Correspondingly, subordinate evaluatory policies must be restructured so that managers will be rewarded (or at least not penalized) for making investments and incurring operating costs related to the so called "nonproductive" assets.

In congruence with this formalization of company policy, it is also suggested that an organizational structure be established for dealing with environmental decisions. At the corporate level, it is suggested that an "environmental committee" be established to oversee and monitor all the company's environmental projects. Many of the case study companies

---

[9]"National Total Annual Costs of Pollution, 1968," in *The Cost of Air Pollution Damages: A Status Report*, U.S. Department of Health, Education, and Welfare (Washington: Government Printing Office, July, 1970).

[10]See, for instance "Sixth Annual Quality Index," *National Wildlife*, Volume 13, No. 2 (February-March, 1975) pp. 3-10.

have established such a committee and found it to be very valuable. This committee should be headed by a top-level executive responsible for environmental affairs (preferably a vice-president). The committee should be charged with coordinating major projects, authorizing necessary appropriations, and establishing timetables for completion. It also should keep up-to-date on available alternative technologies, changes in laws, and problem areas which may be developing. In addition, the vice-president for environmental affairs should deal with policy questions involving federal and state agencies. At the plant or division level, an individual, perhaps titled "environmental coordinator," should be charged with the responsibility of knowing the specifics for compliance with state and federal pollution control laws and for dealing with these agencies concerning operating procedures. The coordinator who will report to the vice-president for environmental affairs should also be responsible for monitoring pollution control costs and for coordinating the environmental and accounting information needed to evaluate alternatives and satisfy the requirements of taxation agencies concerning pollution control bond financing and accelerated amortization deductions. Depending on the size of the company, this coordinator could be assisted by production, engineering, and research and development personnel.

It is suggested that pollution control investments be evaluated as traditional capital investments, with certain modifications. Requests for authorizations for such projects should originate at the plant level and be channeled through the environmental coordinator. An environmental investment capital request form (to be discussed later) should be prepared at this level with, if necessary, assistance from the centralized environmental committee. This report should be sent to the environmental committee for review and approval, after which it should be sent through the traditional capital investment approval channels.

Environmental Investments Planning

The classical economic approach applied to the evaluation of environmental expenditures is to select the point at which marginal costs equal marginal benefits, which is also the point at which there is the maximum difference between total costs and benefits. It is typical, at least in the short run, for an individual company to bear much of the total cost of environmental activity, whereas little of the total benefit accrues directly to the company. Consequently, corporate managers committed to profit maximization in the short or intermediate run are likely to choose to engage in environmental activities which are less than the optimum for society. Committed or concerned companies may choose a higher level of environmental activity than others because of their perception of greater company benefits or because of a conscious altruistic objective. As long as the benefits are perceived by the company to be less than those of society,

EXHIBIT 19

ENVIRONMENTAL CAPITAL INVESTMENT REQUEST

I. **Description:**

II. **Non-monetary Benefits:**

	Quantitative	Non-quantitative

Internal

   Development of salable processes
   Reduced turnover
   Ability to attract new employees
   Reduced absenteeism
   Improved employee efficiency

External (water)

   Public water supply
   Recreational facilities
   Fish & wildlife support
   Aesthetics
   Health
   Overall impact

External (air)

   Health
   Agricultural vegetation
   Wild vegetation
   Property damage
   Wildlife support
   Aesthetics
   Overal impact

III. **Annual Monetary Benefits and Costs:**

	Year 1	Year 2	n

A. **Monetary Benefits:**

    Recyclable raw materials
    Energy production
    By-product sales
    Other

    Total Monetary Benefits

B. **Monetary Costs:**
   (from cost scorecard)

    Total Monetary Costs

    Net Cash Flows Before Taxes (A-B)
    —Depreciation (or CPCF amortization)
    Net Income Before Taxes
    —Income Taxes
    Net Income After Taxes
    +Depreciation (or CPCF amortization)
    Net Cash Flow After Taxes

IV. **Initial Costs** (cash outflows):

   Costs:

   Life of Project:_____

V. **Methods:**

   Net Present Value
   Internal Rate of Return
   Accounting Rate of Return
   Payback

and altruistic motivation does not fill the gap, a role exists for government. Government may enact direct subsidies or tax concessions to increase the benefits and/or decrease the costs to the company, or it may engage directly in environmental activity in order to approach the societal optimum.

It should be recognized that management's perceptions that the company's costs and benefits are different from those of society do not necessarily result from differing attitudes but are a result of the differing constituencies involved. However, in the long run, society bears all the costs of environmental activity and receives all the benefits. For example, the company may eventually pass on all the costs of its environmental activity to its customers in the form of higher prices for its goods or services.

Unfortunately, the current state of knowledge is insufficient to determine all the environmental benefits and costs either for society or the company. This is an area where continuing research to improve upon and refine existing rudimentary models and to extend these models to include newly developing measurement techniques will be particularly beneficial. Currently the most that a company can expect is that it can evaluate individual investment opportunities by using capital budgeting evaluation techniques modified for the specific problems of environmental investments. All the case study companies used some form of capital budgeting for evaluating environmental investments.

Environmental Capital Request Form. A special "environmental capital request" form should be designed to facilitate evaluation of environmental capital budgeting proposals. For ease of understanding, such a form should be as similar as is feasible to the usual company investment request forms. Traditionally, companies have evaluated capital projects by using several different techniques including the present value, the internal rate of return, the accounting rate of return, and the payback method. Many companies compute all four methods. A suggested form shown in Exhibit 19 incorporates these methods.

The first section deals with a description of the project. Here, the reasons for undertaking the project should be explicitly stated. Included should be a general discussion of the affected pollution control laws, relations with the various regulatory agencies, and a timetable for completion.

The next section consists of a summary of the non-monetary benefits. Significant emphasis should be given to those benefits because they may represent the most important factors of the investment. The non-monetary benefits should be obtained from the benefits scorecard discussed in an earlier section. These would include internal benefits, such as the development of salable processes, the reduction of turnover, the increased ability to attract new employees, the reduction of absenteeism, and the improvement of employee efficiency. External benefits might include improvements in public water supply, recreational facilities, fish and wildlife support, vegetation, aesthetics, and health. These should be summarized on either a quantitative or descriptive basis.

The third section is titled "Annual Monetary Benefits and Costs." The annual monetary benefits should be ascertained from the benefits scorecard as discussed earlier. Generally these benefits would include savings due to recycled materials, savings as a result of energy production, and cash inflows from by-product sales. Offsetting these monetary benefits would be the annual cash flows incurred as ascertained from the cost scorecard. As discussed earlier, the primary operating costs would include equipment operating costs, additional production costs, maintenance costs, disposal costs, monitoring costs, and miscellaneous costs (depreciation costs should be excluded because these are not cash flows). In the final year of the project, exit costs should also be included. Reducing the benefits by all these cash outflows yields the annual net cash flow before taxes. This amount should be reduced by the depreciation or Certified Pollution Control Facility accelerated amortization (limited to five years) taken for *tax* purposes, resulting in the net income subject to taxes. Deducting the income taxes (computed by multiplying the marginal tax rate by the taxable net income) yields the net income after taxes. Adding the tax depreciation back to the net income after taxes gives the net cash flow from the project.

The fourth section consists of the estimated initial costs (cash outflows) and the estimated life of the project. Initial cash outflows as itemized on the cost scorecard include land, equipment, engineering, research and development, and miscellaneous costs. These costs should be reduced by any applicable investment credit.

Methods of Analysis

Four methods may be utilized to analyze the investment. Two, the net present value method and the internal rate of return method, are variations of the discounted cash flow technique. This technique recognizes explicitly the time value of money and generally is considered to be the best technique for the evaluation of capital investments.

For the present value method, estimates are made of the amounts and timing of initial and subsequent investments, amounts and timing of operating cash flows, the economic life, the end-of-life salvage value, and a required rate of return. All the cash flows over the economic life are discounted to the present, using the required rate of return. Generally, if the present value is positive, the project is desirable; if negative, it is undesirable. The net present value also can be converted to a profitability index by dividing it by the cash investment.

The internal rate of return method incorporates all of the same variables. Rather than discounting the cash flows using a required rate of re-

EXHIBIT 20

SELECTED MODIFICATIONS OF CAPITAL INVESTMENT ANALYSIS FOR ENVIRONMENTAL INVESTMENTS

It is assumed that the company has a 10 percent weighted average cost of capital computed as follows:

Source of Capital	Amount	Cost
Bonds	$3 Million	8%
Equity	$6 Million	13%

Tax rate = 50%

Weighted average cost of capital: $\frac{(\$3m \times 4\%) + (\$6m \times 13\%)}{\$9m} = 10\%$

The company is considering an environmental investment with the following characteristics:

Initial cost	$1 Million
Annual net cash inflow	$135,800
Life	10 years

Based upon the above information and assuming the company uses typical capital sources, the criteria for evaluating the investment are:

Internal rate of return for the environmental investment = 6%
Net present value (using 10% discount rate) = $(165,568)

MODIFICATIONS TO THE EVALUATION OF THE ENVIRONMENTAL PROJECT

A. Modifications for Reduced Interest Rate

It is assumed that the investment is financed by the use of pollution control bonds with a 4% interest rate

(1) Alternative I: Subtract interest savings from cash inflows

Annual interest saving = (8%-4%) × $1 Million
= $40,000

After tax annual interest saving = $40,000 × (1 − .50)
= $20,000

Annual net cash inflow plus interest   = $155,800

Internal rate of return = 9%

Net present value (using 10% discount rate) = $(42,676)

While still not meeting the economic criteria, the subtraction of the interest savings makes the investment more desirable—the net present value increased by $122,892, and the internal rate of return from 6% to 9%.

(2) Alternative II: Compute new weighted average cost of capital

Source of Capital	Amount	Cost
Bonds	$3 Million	8%
Pollution control bonds	$1 Million	4%
Equity	$6 Million	13%

Net weighted average cost of capital:

$$\frac{(\$3m \times 4\%) + (\$1m \times 2\%) + (\$6m \times 13\%)}{\$10m} = 9.2\%$$

Net Present Value (Using 9.2% discount rate) = $(136,102)

This method again makes the investment more favorable since the net present value increased by $29,466, and the required rate of return is reduced to 9.2% from 10%, as compared to the internal rate of return on the investment of 6%.

B. Modification for Non-Monetary Measurement of Benefits

Use of lower rate for evaluation of project (this example ignores the reduced interest rate on pollution control bonds)

Weighted average cost of capital = 10%
Assumed environmental target rate = 5%

Net present value (using 5% discount rate) = $48,607

This method produces a positive net present value, making the project desirable because the environmental target rate is exceeded.

turn, an internal rate of return, which makes the net present value of the project equal to zero, is calculated. Generally, if the internal rate of return exceeds the required rate of return, the project is desirable.

Three modifications should be considered in applying these methods to environmental expenditure analysis. The first deals with Certified Pollution Control Facility amortization and its effect upon income taxes. If the company elects to use this accelerated amortization over five years, this deduction should be utilized on the environmental investment request in lieu of the usual depreciation.

The second modification deals with interest charges. Typically the financing of an investment is treated separately from the accept/reject decision. As a result, annual cash outflows for interest are disregarded in the discounted cash flow technique. However, in the environmental investment, a specific type of financing is available. "Pollution control" bonds which are tax exempt and therefore carry an interest rate several points below regular bonds may be used to finance these projects. If a firm elects to finance an environmental project via these lower interest bonds, then an "interest opportunity savings" results. These interest savings might be treated as cash inflows for discounting purposes. Alternatively, the interest charges may continue to be excluded from the cash flow computation but reflected in the use of a lower required rate of return. These two alternatives are illustrated in Exhibit 20.

A third modification involves a reduction in the required rate of return for environmental investments as compared to that rate required for economic investments. A reduced rate of return may be acceptable because all of the benefits related to an environmental project are not measured in monetary terms and because it is felt implicitly that if the nonmonetary measurements were included, their cash inflows would make up the difference between the traditional rate and the lower rate. This approach also is illustrated in Exhibit 20. However, the use of this technique would be inappropriate when the analysis includes the measurement of all benefits in monetary terms (as discussed in other sections of this chapter) because it would result in a double-counting of these benefits.

Although less refined than the discounted cash flow method, some managers use the accounting rate of return method. Here, an accounting rate of return is computed by dividing the expected increase in future annual income by the expected increase in the required investment. Refinements which may be made to this basic calculation include averaging of the income and the investment, allocation of working capital to the investment base, and computations on a before and after tax basis. When computing the accounting rate of return for the environmental investment request, care should be taken to adjust for any differences between the depreciation shown for tax purposes and that to be charged for accounting purposes.

Finally the payback, which is the time it will take to recover the initial investment, may be computed. This entails dividing the initial cash outflows by the annual incremental cash inflows resulting from the project. While not measuring profitability, it does produce a measure of the liquidity of the project.

The application of these methods to the evaluation of environmental investments presents special problems. Since the non-monetary benefits are not additive to the monetary benefits, nor are they necessarily additive among themselves, difficulties arise concerning an overall evaluation.

One method by which the decision maker can give explicit consideration to the relationship between the monetary and non-monetary benefits is to consider the value which would have to attach to the non-monetary benefits in order to make the project desirable according to the normal evaluation criterion. It may be obvious immediately that the value of the non-monetary benefits clearly either does or does not exceed the amount required to make the project acceptable. Therefore it is only in the "gray" area where the non-monetary benefits are of an amount which may put the decision on the borderline of the accept/reject criterion that further investigation is warranted.

An alternative approach for dealing with the non-monetary benefits is for consideration to be given to desirable or acceptable trade-offs between the various benefits. The following are some examples of the kinds of trade-offs involved.

(1) Reduction of pollution to a certain level will cost a given amount. Further reduction will cost an additional amount. A decision to invest the additional amount indicates an implicit trade-off between the incremental investment and pollution. Is such a trade-off desirable or acceptable? For example, suppose an expenditure of $1 million will provide a biological oxygen demand (BOD) level of nine parts per million. Expenditure of an additional $300,000 will reduce the level to six p.p.m. A decision to invest the additional $300,000 implies that a trade-off of $100,000 per part per million is desirable, and rejection of the additional investment implies that such a trade-off is undesirable.

(2) A company may be deciding between two discretionary investments as follows:

    (a) Reduce discharge into the air by 10 tons/day—cost $10,000
    (b) Reduce discharge into the water by 5 tons/day—cost $6,000

Acceptance of the first investment implies that an expenditure of $1,000 per ton per day for reducing air pollution is more desirable than one of $1,200 per ton per day for reducing water pollution. Or put another way, the reduction of total effluent by an additional five tons per day is worth an expenditure of $4,000 or $800 per ton. Of course acceptance of the second investment would imply just the opposite kinds of relationships.

(3) An investment for pollution abatement usually involves increased use of energy. Although the company knows the cost to it of additional energy use, what is the impact on the use of scarce resources? An environmental investment implies a certain relationship between pollution and energy use (i.e., the removal of one ton of air pollution is worth the use of X tons of coal for energy).

It is recognized that giving explicit consideration to the trade-offs between the non-monetary benefits does not necessarily make the decision process any easier. However, such consideration should lead the decision maker to a more rational decision. As techniques and information improve, it should be possible to go beyond the consideration of the trade-offs implied by a decision to the development of normative values for the trade-offs. An example of this is the development by the Department of Health, Education and Welfare of the costs of reducing air pollution.[11] The figures developed are the total costs to society to clean up various types of pollution rather than measures of the benefits to society of cleaning up. However, if one is willing to assume that the benefits at least exceed the costs, then the figures could be used by individual companies as crude measures of the trade-offs among various types of pollution.

Since many of the factors (e.g., costs, benefits, cost of capital) included in the evaluation of environmental activity are difficult to measure, it may be useful for the decision maker to consider how changes in the values of the factors might affect the decision. The evaluation of environmental investments involves two kinds of uncertainty. First, because of the newness of much of the technology of pollution control, there is uncertainty involved on the physical level. What pollution control effect will certain equipment have? Second, there is uncertainty regarding the numbers that should be attached to the physical activities so that comparisons can be made.

The many factors involved in environmental decisions and their potential interactions suggest that a selection must be made of the factors and particular combinations which appear likely to have the most signifi-

---

[11] The Second Report of the Secretary of Health, Education and Welfare, in compliance with PL 90-148, *The Clean Air Act,* as amended, March, 1970, in Seidler and Seidler, *op. cit.,* p. 288.

cant effect upon the decision and which may be investigated at the least cost. Unfortunately, no *ex ante* ranking of important factors exists. At best, a suggestion may be made as to what criteria should be used to develop such a ranking.

Each factor may be ranked on the basis of the following three criteria: (1) how uncertain are the estimates of the factor, (2) how much does the factor interact in a complementary manner with the other factors, and (3) what is the relative magnitude of the value of this factor as compared to the other factors?

An example of the application of these criteria to an environmental analysis is provided by some previous research performed by one of the authors.[12] The factors and the evaluation of the three criteria for each factor are summarized in Exhibit 21.

EXHIBIT 21

THE ANALYSIS OF UNCERTAIN FACTORS IN THE ENVIRONMENTAL ACTIVITY DECISION

Factor	Uncertainty	Complementary Interaction	Relative Magnitude
Investment	High	Medium	High
Certification Percentage	Medium	High	High
Liquidation Value of Plant & Equip.	High	High	?
Cost of Capital	Medium	High	NA
Operating Costs	Low	High	Medium
Price of Product	Low	High	NA

NA = not applicable

As a result of this evaluation, the analysis concentrated on the size of the investment, the percentage of the investment classified as a certified pollution control facility, the liquidation value, and the cost of capital.

It should be emphasized that when decisions are made in which nonquantifiable factors play an important part, the value judgements of the decision maker become correspondingly more important in the decision process. The importance of such value judgments can be minimized only

---

[12]Loren A. Nikolai, "Accounting Analysis for Pollution Control," (Unpublished Ph.D. Dissertation, University of Minnesota, Minneapolis, 1973).

when accepted, reliable, and comparable measures of all the benefits of investments in pollution control equipment are developed.

Environmental Operational Planning and Control

In addition to long-term capital budgeting, companies also engage in operational planning and control. This entails the establishment of goals, the quantification of these goals in the form of budgets, analysis of deviations of actual results from planned results, and the application of responsibility accounting. Responsibility accounting is the process of identifying the manager who has the authority and control over each cost and revenue. A manager is said to have "profit" responsibility if he is charged with the planning and control of both revenues and costs. Similarly, a manager has "cost" responsibility when he is concerned only with costs. Typically, then, the overall company budget is broken down into "responsibility center" budgets with the appropriate manager responsible for the development of and control over the quantified plans related to his managerial area.

With the emphasis on extending corporate responsibility beyond the traditional profit objective to include social objectives, it is desirable to extend the responsibility accounting concept to include "social" responsibility or more specifically "environmental responsibility accounting." Under this concept, each manager would be charged with the planning of his environmental costs and benefits as well as the planning of his operating costs and revenues. In this way, direction can be given to the attainment of company environmental responsibility objectives.

The environmental benefits scorecard illustrated in Exhibit 16 and the environmental cost scorecard illustrated in Exhibit 15 might be utilized in the operational planning stages for environmental activities. Planned annual internal and external environmental benefits should be identified and measured on either a monetary, quantitative but not monetary, or a non-quantitative basis. In a like manner, planned annual environmental costs should be identified and measured. This planning process will serve to direct each manager's attention to the expected benefits received and costs incurred as a result of intended environmental activities undertaken to meet the company's environmental social responsibility.

Control is closely related to responsibility accounting and performance evaluation. It is desirable for companies to measure the actual costs incurred and the benefits obtained from environmental activities according to the categories used in the planning process. This will facilitate adjustment of normal control procedures in order to incorporate the environmental activities. Control procedures are likely to vary from company to company so that specific recommendations may have limited generalizability. However, most companies will engage in systematic variance analysis as well as performance evaluation.

Variance analysis involves a comparison of actual performance with planned performance in order to identify deviations. The overall objective is to isolate significant controllable deviations and their related causes so that corrective action may be taken to bring actual performance into line with planned performance. Certainly this type of control procedure could be adapted for use concerning environmental performance. One possibility would be to develop three (or more) "environmental activity" variances, such as an "environmental discharge" variance, an "environmental effectiveness" variance, and an "environmental efficiency" variance. These could be applied to each department and might be expressed as shown below:

Environmental Discharge Variance	= Standard Level of Pollutant Discharge—Actual Level of Pollutant Discharge
Environmental Effectiveness Variance	= Desired Level of Environmental Benefits—Actual Level of Environmental Benefits
Environmental Efficiency Variance	= Standard Cost for Actual Discharge Level—Actual Cost for Actual Discharge Level

Each company can modify these variances to fit into its own variance format, including the likelihood of having "descriptive" variances where quantitative measurements are not ascertainable. By establishing and implementing such variances, the company can stimulate a manager to concentrate upon the environmental segment of his responsibility.

In addition to the use of variance analysis, each manager's longer term performance typically is reviewed. Consideration should be given to the impact of environmental activities upon departmental performance criteria. Again, modifications of performance evaluation are likely to vary from company to company. However, each company must consider not only the impact upon the performance measure itself, but also the impact upon the motivation of the manager. For instance, many companies will use some form of return on investment (ROI) to evaluate each departmental manager. The ROI is computed by dividing the department's net income by its share of the company's asset base. The company may compute an annual ROI and compare this to other managers' current performance as well as to the specific manager's past performance. Environmental activities will impact upon the ROI in several ways. First, environmental investments or operational costs may not contribute to the department's monetary net income. Second, different departments may require different amounts (and percentages) of assets tied up in environmental investments. Therefore, in order to improve comparability across time and across departments, it might be desirable to factor out of the denominator that portion of the assets tied up in environmental investments, and out of the numerator that portion of environmental period costs not associated with the production of net income. If these environmental period costs and investments are factored out of the traditional ROI, then, perhaps, further annual performance measures might be developed. Examples might include a comparison of yearly environmental operating costs to environmental assets, the development of a rate of return which compares environmental benefits to the environmental investment base, or a ratio of annual environmental benefits to operating costs.

Such modifications also are likely to encourage the manager toward achievement of the company's environmental objective. Several of the case studies revealed that department managers were reluctant to make investments in pollution control equipment because it would have a detrimental effect upon their ROI. A separate evaluation of the environmental activity may help the manager to develop a positive attitude toward such activities. Furthermore, establishment of environmental performance measures may assist in the achievement of the company's social responsibility objectives.

A problem arises because neither the plans nor the actual measurements are entirely in comparable monetary units. Some of the benefits will be on either a quantitative but non-monetary, or a non-quantitative basis and so total performance cannot be evaluated by a single figure. There may be a danger that managers will consider the monetary figures more important than the non-monetary simply because they typically are more used in budgeting. However this tendency should be avoided to assure rational decision making in the social responsibility area.

The environmental benefits and environmental cost scorecards should be utilized for the control of both the project and operational plans. However, the companies that participated in the case studies indicated that they find it difficult to justify the effort involved in identifying, recording, and analyzing these costs and benefits purely for internal control purposes. Admittedly, for many companies it is likely that in the short run, the cost of collecting this information will exceed the benefits obtained by the company. Two factors tend to mitigate the importance of this argument against such measurement. First, as the measurement activity becomes institutionalized, the cost of collecting the information should become less, and therefore, the likelihood of the benefits exceeding the costs becomes greater. Secondly, the measurement of the actual costs and benefits will satisfy directly certain external reporting requirements (such as those of the SEC and the EPA), which in turn should lead to indirect benefits to the individual company.

Summary and Conclusions

In this chapter the nature of environmental costs and benefits are discussed along with their usefulness for planning and control.

Various approaches to the definition of environmental costs are discussed. The authors recommend that environmental costs should include only traceable incremental costs incurred for environmental projects. When costs are incurred to produce both environmental and economic benefits, the environmental costs should be distinguished from those incurred to produce economic benefits. The practical problems involved in the separation of joint costs need resolution so that companies have practical guidelines to follow.

Costs associated with environmental activities are classified into three groups. Initial costs, which are incurred in order to get the activity online, include land, equipment, engineering, research and development and miscellaneous costs. Operating costs, which are incurred while the activity is operating, include equipment operating, additional production, maintenance, disposal, monitoring, depreciation, and miscellaneous costs. Finally, exit costs are those costs which are incurred to close down the activity.

An environmental benefit is defined as a benefit to the environment which results from an expenditure of an environmental cost. Internal environmental benefits directly benefit the company while indirectly benefiting society, whereas external environmental benefits directly benefit society while indirectly benefiting the company.

Internal environmental benefits are categorized as the use of recyclable raw materials, the production of energy, the sale of by-products, the development of salable processes, the improvements of working conditions including reduced turnover, increased ability to attract new employees, reduced absenteeism and improved employee efficiency, and the improvement of the company's "good citizenship" reputation.

Because external benefits are important to recognize but may be difficult to measure in monetary terms, several different non-monetary measurement models are reviewed and their "input variables" identified. The authors recommend that the quantities of reductions in the various polluting substances be identified along with each group of users or uses and ranked in importance. Finally, some sort of common "measurement unit" should be established in order to convey the relative impact upon these users or uses. Examples of external benefits include improvements in public water supply, recreational facilities, fish and wildlife support, vegetation, aesthetics, and health. Additional research on improvements in the measurement of environmental benefits would be beneficial.

Environmental investment and operational planning and control are discussed. A company environmental policy, organizational structure, and capital investment request form are recommended. It is suggested that environmental investments should be evaluated as traditional capital investments, with certain modifications. Consideration should be given to Certified Pollution Control Facility acceleration amortization effects on cash flows, to savings in interest charges due to financing via "pollution control bonds," to the evaluation of non-monetary benefits, and to the effect of changes in the values of the factors on the investment decision.

For operational planning, the authors recommend that the concept of responsibility accounting be extended to include environmental responsibility. In this way, the company can direct each manager's attention to the expected benefits received and costs incurred as a result of intended environmental activity for which he is responsible and which is undertaken to achieve the company's environmental social responsibility.

For control purposes, it is suggested that the company measure the actual costs incurred and the benefits obtained from environmental investments according to the categories discussed earlier. Modifications of normal control procedures are discussed, including environmental variance analysis and adjustments to performance evaluation.

Appendix

APPENDIX

THE MEASUREMENT OF ENVIRONMENTAL IMPACTS

A Questionnaire Prepared By

Loren A. Nikolai, Assistant Professor of Accounting
John D. Bazley, Assistant Professor of Accounting
R. Lee Brummet, Willard J. Graham, Professor of Business Administration
All of the University of North Carolina at Chapel Hill

Introduction

This questionnaire is the first stage of a three-stage study being sponsored by the National Association of Accountants. It is expected that the results of the study will be published by and disseminated through the NAA.

The purpose of this questionnaire is to determine the measurement techniques utilized by your company to evaluate the costs and benefits associated with corporate actions which impact upon the environment and the resulting effect upon corporate decision-making. We are interested in such actions whether or not undertaken to meet legal requirements or to increase efficiency, but only to the extent that such actions benefit the environment over and above meeting the basic economic needs of the company. For example, the costs and benefits of scrubbers, waste treatment facilities, etc. incorporated into a new plant are of concern, but not the total cost of the new plant. It should be completed by an individual who is both knowledgeable of corporate efforts to measure relevant costs and benefits associated with environmental factors and in a position to judge the impact of such measurements on company decision-making.

In this questionnaire, "your company" refers to the company to which this questionnaire is addressed (or relevant "segment" thereof) plus any domestic subsidiaries. "Environmental factors" refers to such aspects as air, water, and land pollution, aesthetics, and the consumption, recycling, or disposal of non-replaceable physical resources.

Please respond to the questions as completely as possible. Most may be answered by a check mark or number on an appropriate line. If you feel that your answers to the questions do not fit the available responses, please write in beside the question whatever response you feel is appropriate. In addition, at the end of Part III, question 26 requests your comments concerning items which you feel may be of interest to us but which we failed to identify clearly. Please note that there are questions on both sides of each page.

The questionnaire is coded for follow-up purposes only. We would like to reassure you that your responses will be held confidential. If you wish to receive a copy of the results, please indicate below.

_____Yes, we wish to receive a copy of the questionnaire results. Please send the results to:

Part I: General Information

1. Does your company have an individual within the organization who has, as a major portion of his (her) responsibility, a concern with the measurements of the costs and benefits associated with environmental factors and the resulting effect upon corporate decision-making?

    Yes_____   No_____

    If your answer is "yes," please check one of the below and list his (her) title:

    _____Corporate Vice President or above
    List his (her) title here _____

    _____Below corporate Vice President
    List his (her) title here _____

2. Please indicate the title of the person who does complete this questionnaire.

        Title _____

3. If you wish to limit your answers to a particular segment or project of your company, please provide a general description of that segment or project (i.e. product or process description, S.I.C. number, etc.).

4. Indicate the degree to which your company measures the costs associated with its activities in each of the following environmental categories by placing on the line corresponding to each category, one of the following numbers: 0 (none), 1 (minor), 2 (moderate), or 3 (major).

        Water _____
        Air _____
        Land _____
        Noise _____
        Other (list) _____

5. Indicate the significance of the contribution that each of the following functional areas has made as your company has progressed in its attempts to make measurements, in monetary terms, of the costs and benefits associated with environmental factors by placing on the line corresponding to each area, one of the following numbers: 0 (none), 1 (minor), 2 (moderate), or 3 (major).

        Manufacturing _____
        Engineering _____
        Research & Development _____
        Legal _____
        Accounting _____
        Marketing _____
        Other (list) _____ _____

Part II: Costs Associated with Environmental Factors

5. **Additional Initial Costs**

   Questions 6 through 10 deal specifically with the additional initial costs incurred and separately categorized because of a concern with the effect of your company's planned or actual activities upon environmental factors. For purposes of this questionnaire, two of the categories of costs are defined as follows:

   equipment costs—additional capital asset, installation, and testing costs

   disruption costs—additional opportunity costs and any "down-time" costs

6. Referring to the definitions above, indicate whether your company measures, in monetary terms, the following categories of additional initial costs by placing a check mark in the appropriate column(s).

	Yes	No
Research and development costs		
Equipment costs		
Disruption costs		
Legal costs		

7. For any of the costs for which your answer to Question 6 is "yes," indicate the impact that each of the following reasons had on the decision to undertake such cost measurements by placing on each relevant line, one of the following numbers: 0 (none), 1 (minor), 2 (moderate), or 3 (major).

To provide information:	R&D	Eqpmt	Dsrpt	Legal
To meet legal requirements				
For external reporting				
To obtain pollution control tax advantages				
For decision-making concerning self-imposed social responsibilities				
For decision-making concerning externally-induced social responsibilities				
Other (list) _____				

8. For any of the costs for which your answer to Question 6 is "yes," indicate the impact of the use of such measurements upon your company's decision-making by placing on each relevant line, one of the following numbers: 0 (none), 1 (minor), 2 (moderate), or 3 (major).

	R&D	Eqpmt	Dsrpt	Legal
Impact upon company decision-making	___	___	___	___

9. For any of the costs for which your answer to Question 6 is "no," indicate the impact that each of the following reasons had on the decision *not* to undertake such measurements by placing on each relevant line, one of the following numbers: 0 (none), 1 (minor), 2 (moderate), or 3 (major).

	R&D	Eqpmt	Dsrpt	Legal
Not required legally	___	___	___	___
Not desirable use of monetary resources	___	___	___	___
Not desirable use of personnel resources	___	___	___	___
No monetary resources to do so	___	___	___	___
No personnel resources to do so	___	___	___	___
No techniques available to do so	___	___	___	___
Other (list) _____	___	___	___	___

10. For any of the costs for which your answer to *Question 6* is "no," indicate whether and how your company measures those additional initial costs in non-monetary terms by placing, on the line(s) corresponding to each cost, a check mark(s) in the appropriate column.

Type of Measurement:

	Quantitative	Non Quantitative	Not Measured
Research and development costs	___	___	___
Equipment costs	___	___	___
Disruption costs	___	___	___
Legal costs	___	___	___

B. **Additional Operating Costs**

Questions 11 through 15 deal specifically with the additional operating costs incurred and separately categorized because of a concern with the effect of your company's planned or actual activities upon environmental factors. These costs, for the purposes of this questionnaire, are defined as follows:

production costs —additional materials, direct labor and direct overhead

monitoring costs —additional costs of labor, supplies, etc. to monitor your degree of compliance with predetermined acceptable levels of pollution

recycling costs —additional costs incurred as a result of recycling physical resources

avoidance costs —the costs of cleaning up a natural resource used as an input into your production process

disposal costs —costs incurred that are associated with the adequate disposal of waste products which are not recycled

maintenance costs —costs of labor, supplies, etc. to keep your pollution control equipment functioning properly

11. Referring to the definitions above, indicate whether your company measures, in monetary terms, the following categories of additional operating costs by placing a check mark in the appropriate column(s).

	Yes	No
Production costs	____	____
Monitoring costs	____	____
Recycling costs	____	____
Avoidance costs	____	____
Disposal costs	____	____
Maintenance costs	____	____

12. For any of the costs for which your answer to *Question 11* is "yes," indicate the impact that each of the following reasons had on the decision to undertake such cost measurements by placing on each relevant line, one of the following numbers: 0 (none), 1 (minor), 2 (moderate), or 3 (major).

	Prod	Mntrg	Recyc	Avoid	Disp	Maint
To provide information:						
To meet legal requirements	___	___	___	___	___	___
For external reporting	___	___	___	___	___	___
To obtain pollution control tax advantages	___	___	___	___	___	___
For decision-making concerning self-imposed social responsibilities	___	___	___	___	___	___
For decision-making concerning externally-induced social responsibilities	___	___	___	___	___	___
Other (list) _____	___	___	___	___	___	___

13. For any of the costs for which your answer to Question 11 is "yes," indicate the impact of such measurements upon your company's decision-making by placing on each relevant line, one of the following numbers: 0 (none), 1 (minor), 2 (moderate), or 3 (major).

	Prod	Mntrg	Recyc	Avoid	Disp	Maint
Impact upon company decision-making	___	___	___	___	___	___

14. For any of the costs for which your answer to *Question 11* is "no," indicate the impact that each of the following reasons had on the decision *not* to undertake such measurements by placing on each relevant line, one of the following numbers: 0 (none), 1 (minor), 2 (moderate), or 3 (major).

	Prod	Mntrg	Recyc	Avoid	Disp	Maint
Not required legally	___	___	___	___	___	___
Not desirable use of monetary resources	___	___	___	___	___	___
Not desirable use of personnel resources	___	___	___	___	___	___
No monetary resources to do so	___	___	___	___	___	___
No personnel resources to do so	___	___	___	___	___	___
No techniques available to do so	___	___	___	___	___	___
Other (list) ___	___	___	___	___	___	___

15. For any of the costs for which your answer to *Question 11* is "no," indicate whether and how your company measures those additional operating costs in non-monetary terms by placing, on the line(s) corresponding to each cost, a check mark(s) in the appropriate column.

	Type of Measurement:		
	Quantitative	Non Quantitative	Not Measured
Production costs	___	___	___
Monitoring costs	___	___	___
Recycling costs	___	___	___
Avoidance costs	___	___	___
Disposal costs	___	___	___
Maintenance costs	___	___	___

C. **Additional Indirect Costs**

Questions 16 through 20 deal specifically with the additional costs which are not directly associated with the production process but which are incurred and separately categorized because of a concern with the effect of your company's planned or actual activities upon environmental factors. For purposes of this questionnaire, these costs are defined as follows:

aesthetic costs —additional costs incurred to design, locate, and maintain facilities in conformance with aesthetically pleasing architecture and landscaping

restoration costs —additional costs incurred to voluntarily restore the removal site of the natural resource to an environmentally satisfactory state

image promotion costs —costs incurred to communicate a realistic and positive image of environmental concern by the company

16. Referring to the definitions above, indicate whether your company measures, in monetary terms, the following categories of additional indirect costs by placing a check mark in the appropriate column(s).

	Yes	No
Aesthetic costs	____	____
Restoration costs	____	____
Image promotion costs	____	____
Other (list)_____	____	____

17. For any of the costs for which your answer to *Question 16* is "yes," indicate the impact that each of the following reasons had on the decision to undertake such cost measurements by placing on each relevant line, one of the following numbers: 0 (none), 1 (minor), 2 (moderate), or 3 (major).

			Image	
To provide information:	Aest	Restr	Prmn	Other
To meet legal requirements	____	____	____	____
For external reporting	____	____	____	____
To obtain pollution control tax advantages	____	____	____	____
For decision-making concerning self-imposed social responsibilities	____	____	____	____
For decision-making concerning externally-induced social responsibilities	____	____	____	____
Other (list)_____	____	____	____	____

18. For any of the costs for which your answer to *Question 16* is "yes," indicate the impact of such measurements upon your company's decision-making by placing on each relevant line, one of the following numbers: 0 (none), 1 (minor), 2 (moderate), or 3 (major).

	Aest	Restr	Image Prmn	Other
Impact upon corporate decision-making	____	____	____	____

19. For any of the costs for which your answer to *Question 16* is "no," indicate the impact that each of the following reasons had on the decision *not* to undertake such measurements by placing on each relevant line, one of the following numbers: 0 (none), 1 (minor), 2 (moderate), or 3 (major).

	Aest	Restr	Image Prmn	Other
Not required legally	____	____	____	____
Not desirable use of monetary resources	____	____	____	____
Not desirable use of personnel resources	____	____	____	____
No monetary resources to do so	____	____	____	____
No personnel resources to do so	____	____	____	____
No techniques to do so	____	____	____	____
Other (list) _____	____	____	____	____

20. For any of the costs for which your answer to *Question 16* is "no," indicate whether and how your company measures those additional indirect costs in non-monetary terms by placing, on the line(s) corresponding to each cost, a check mark(s) in the appropriate column.

Type of Measurement:

	Quantitative	Non Quantitative	Not Measured
Aesthetic costs	____	____	____
Restoration costs	____	____	____
Image promotion costs	____	____	____
Other (list) _____	____	____	____

Part III: Benefits Associated With Environmental Factors

Questions 21 through 25 deal specifically with the additional benefits derived and separately categorized as a result of a concern with the effect of your company's planned or actual activities upon environmental factors. For purposes of this questionnaire, the *conservation of scarce physical resources* should include either reduced use or recycling.

21. Indicate whether your company measures, in monetary terms, the following categories of additional benefits by placing a check mark in the appropriate column.

	Yes	No
Reduced production costs	___	___
Avoidance of legal costs and penalties	___	___
Improved public image	___	___
Improved employee satisfaction	___	___
Reduction in pollution caused by the company's activities	___	___
Reduction in pollution caused by the use of the company's products	___	___
Conservation of scarce physical resources	___	___

22. For any of the benefits for which your answer to *Question 21* is "yes," indicate the impact that each of the following reasons had on the decision to undertake such benefit measurements by placing on each relevant line, one of the following numbers: 0 (none), 1 (minor) 2 (moderate), and 3 (major).

	Reduce Prod Cost	Avoid Legal Cost	Impr Public Image	Impr Empl Satis	Reduce Pol By Comp	Reduce Pol By Prod	Consr Phys Resou
To provide information:							
To meet legal requirements	___	___	___	___	___	___	___
For external reporting	___	___	___	___	___	___	___
To obtain pollution control tax advantages	___	___	___	___	___	___	___

	Reduce Prod Cost	Avoid Legal Cost	Impr Public Image	Impr Empl Satis	Reduce Pol By Comp	Reduce Pol By Prod	Consr Phys Resou
For decision-making concerning self-imposed social responsibilties	___	___	___	___	___	___	___
For decision-making concerning externally induced social responsibilities	___	___	___	___	___	___	___
Other (list) ___	___	___	___	___	___	___	___

For any of the benefits for which your answer to *Question 21* is "yes," indicate the impact of such measurements upon your company's decision-making by placing on each relevant line one of the following numbers: 0 (none), 1 (minor), 2 (moderate), or 3 (major).

	Reduce Prod Cost	Avoid Legal Cost	Impr Public Image	Impr Empl Satis	Reduce Pol By Comp	Reduce Pol By Prod	Consr Phys Resou
Impact upon company decision-making	___	___	___	___	___	___	___

24. For any of the benefits for which your answer to *Question 21* is "no," indicate the impact that each of the following reasons had on the decision *not* to undertake such measurements by placing on each relevant line, one of the following numbers: 0 (none), 1 (minor), 2 (moderate), or 3 (major).

	Reduce Prod Cost	Avoid Legal Cost	Impr Public Image	Impr Empl Satis	Reduce Pol By Comp	Reduce Pol By Prod	Consr Phys Resou
Not required legally	_____	_____	_____	_____	_____	_____	_____
Not desirable use of monetary resources	_____	_____	_____	_____	_____	_____	_____
Not desirable use of personnel resources	_____	_____	_____	_____	_____	_____	_____
No monetary resources to do so	_____	_____	_____	_____	_____	_____	_____
No personnel resources to do so	_____	_____	_____	_____	_____	_____	_____
No techniques available to do so	_____	_____	_____	_____	_____	_____	_____
Other (list)_____	_____	_____	_____	_____	_____	_____	_____

25. For any of the benefits for which your answer to *Question 21* is "no," indicate whether and how your company measures those additional company benefits in non-monetary terms by placing, on the line(s) corresponding to each benefit, a check mark(s) in the appropriate column.

Type of Measurement:

	Quantitative	Non Quantitative	Not Measured
Reduced production costs	_____	_____	_____
Avoidance of legal costs and penalties	_____	_____	_____
Improved public image	_____	_____	_____
Improved employee satisfaction	_____	_____	_____

	Non Quantitative	Quantitative	Not Measured
Reduction in pollution caused by the company's activities	_____	_____	_____
Reduction in pollution caused by the use of the company's products	_____	_____	_____
Conservation of scarce physical resources	_____	_____	_____

26. **Additional Information:** Please discuss on a separate sheet of paper any aspects of costs incurred and benefits derived as a result of a concern with the effect of your company's planned or actual activities upon environmental factors which are not covered by the above questions and which you think will be of interest to us.

Part IV: Subsequent Research

The next stage of our research will involve case studies of several firms which are active in the measurement of the costs and benefits associated with environmental factors. The case studies will be designed to determine precisely how individual firms measure the costs and benefits associated with environmental factors and how they incorporate them into their information systems and their decision-making process. This stage will entail in-depth interviews with cooperating firms which have indicated in this questionnaire their interest and ability to undertake such measurements. The personal interview would be conducted with the executive most responsible for measuring the costs and benefits of environmental factors and their effect upon corporate decision-making. This interview is expected to involve a one-day visit by one of the researchers (at each company) sometime in late 1974 or early 1975. A minimal amount of additional time would be spent on written correspondence. If your company is interested in participating in this second stage of the research, we would be greatly appreciative if you would indicate such below.

____Yes, we are interested in participating in the second stage of the study. Title and address of corporate executive to be contacted:

_____
_____
_____
_____

Thank you for your time and effort in completing this questionnaire. Please return this questionnaire in the enclosed self-addressed envelope to:

>Professor Loren A. Nikolai
>School of Business Administration
>University of North Carolina
>Chapel Hill, North Carolina 27514

BIBLIOGRAPHY

Abel, Fred H. and Dennis P. Tihansky. "Methods and Problems of Estimating Water-Quality Benefits," *Journal of the American Water Works Association*, (May, 1974), p. 276-281.

Air Pollution Control Technology and Costs in Nine Areas. National Technical Information Service Report, PB-222 746/OWP, September 30, 1972.

Chesler, L.G., and B.F. Goeller. *The STAR Methodology for Short Haul Transportation: Transportation Impact Assessment*. Prepared for U.S. Department of Transportation, R-1359-DOT. Santa Monica: Rand Corporation, December, 1973.

Commoner, Barry. *The Closing Circle*. New York: Alfred A. Knopf, Inc., 1971.

Dee, Norbert, et. al. *Environmental Evaluation System for Water Resource Planning*. Battelle Columbus Laboratories for Bureau of Reclamation, U.S. Department of the Interior, Washington, 1972.

DeGreene, Kenyon B. *Sociotechnical Systems*. Englewood Cliffs, New Jersey: Prentice-Hall, Inc., 1973.

Deininger, Rolf A. (ed.) *Seminar on the Design of Environmental Information Systems, Katowice, Poland, 1973*. Ann Arbor: Ann Arbor Science Publishers, 1974.

Dinius, S.H. "Social Accounting System for Evaluating Water Resources," *Water Resources Research*, Volume 8, No. 5, October, 1972, p. 1159-1177.

Dolan, Edwin G. *TANSTAFFL, The Economic Strategy for Environmental Crisis*. New York: Holt, Rhinehart and Winston, Inc., 1971.

Environmental Expenditures of the United States Petroleum Industry, 1966-1973. Publication No. 4233. Washington: American Petroleum Institute.

Federal Income Tax Regulation 1.103-8.

Internal Revenue Code of 1954, as amended, Sections 103 and 169.

Jones, P.M.S. "Cost Analysis in the Field of Air Pollution," *Atmospheric Environment*, Volume 7, No. 12 (December, 1973), p. 1191-98.

Jordening, David L. and James K. Allwood. *Research Needs and Priorities: Water Pollution Control Benefits and Costs*. Volume II, U.S. Environmental Protection Agency. Washington: Government Printing Office, 1973.

Lund, Leonard. *Industry Expenditures for Water Pollution Abatement*. New York: The Conference Board, Inc., 1972.

Marstrand, P.K. "Assessing the Intangibles in Water Pollution Control," *International Journal of Environmental Studies*. Volume 5, No. 4, (December, 1973), p. 289-298.

Mergen, Francois (ed.) *Man and His Environment: The Ecological Limits of Optimism*. Yale University: School of Forestry Bulletin No. 76. New Haven: Yale University, 1970.

Nikolai, Loren A. "Accounting Analysis for Pollution Control." Unpublished Ph.D. Dissertation, University of Minnesota, 1973.

Nikolai, Loren A. and Donald E. Pickets. "The Use of 'Certified Pollution Facility' Amortization: An Optimal Strategy?" *Volume II: Contributed Sessions Papers, Fifth Annual Midwest AIDS Conference*, May 10-11, 1974, p. T37-T40.

Peckham, Brian W. *Bibliography of Literature Relating to the Economic and Legal Aspects of Air Pollution*. University of North Carolina, Wilson Library: Chapel Hill, North Carolina, 1971.

Popovich, M.L., L. Duckstein, and C.C. Kisiel. "Cost Effectiveness Analysis of Disposal Systems," *Journal of the Environmental Division* (American Society of Civil Engineers), Volume 99 (October, 1973), p. 577-591.

Prati, L., R. Pavanello, and F. Pesarin. "Assessment of Surface Water Quality by a Single Index of Pollution," *Water Resources Research* (GB), No. 5, 1971, p. 741-751.

Seidler, Lee J. and Lynn L. Seidler. *Social Accounting*. Los Angeles: Melville Publishing Company, 1975.

Selection of Air Pollution Control Equipment. NTIS Report AD-768 115/8WP, July, 1971.

"Sixth Annual Quality Index," *National Wildlife*, Volume 13, No. 2, February-March, 1975.

The Economic Impact of Pollution Control: A Summary of Recent Studies. Washington: Council on Environmental Quality, U.S. Department of Commerce, and the Environmental Protection Agency, March, 1972.

Tihansky, D.P. "Historical Development of Water Pollution Control Cost Functions," *Water Pollution Control Federation Journal*, Volume 46, No. 5, (May, 1974), p. 813-33.

Unger, Samuel G., M. Jarvin Emerson, and David L. Jordening. *State of the Art Review: Water Pollution Control Benefits and Costs.* Volume I, U.S. Environmental Protection Agency. Washington: Government Printing Office, 1973.

U.S. Department of Health, Education and Welfare. "National Total Annual Costs of Pollution, 1968," *The Cost of Air Pollution Damages: A Status Report.* Washington: Government Printing Office, July, 1970.

U.S. Environmental Protection Agency. *Capital and Operating Costs of Pollution Control Equipment Modules.* 2 volumes. (Publication: EPA-R5-73-023 a&b) December, 1973.

NAA Committee on Research

Donald H. Cramer, Chairman
Touche Ross & Company
New York, New York

Morton Backer
University of Massachusetts
Amherst, Massachusetts

Eugene A. Bates
J.I. Case Company
Racine, Wisconsin

Henry L. Clayton, Sr.
Corning Glass Works
Corning, New York

Robert L. Cramer
Florida Gas Company
Winter Park, Florida

Dwight H. Davis
A.O. Smith Corporation
Milwaukee, Wisconsin

Geraldine F. Dominiak
Texas Christian University
Ft. Worth, Texas

Patricia P. Douglas
University of Montana
Missoula, Montana

Kenneth J. Doyle
Price Waterhouse & Co.
Stamford, Connecticut

J. Bernard Eck
May, Zima & Company
Daytona Beach, Florida

James Don Edwards
University of Georgia
Athens, Georgia

William L. Ferrara
Penn. State University
University Park, Pennsylvania

Homer R. Figler
Ernst & Ernst
New York, New York

Glen R. Kellam
The Upjohn Company
Kalamazoo, Michigan

Willis A. Leonhardi
Arthur Andersen & Co.
Chicago, Illinois

Ray L. Longenecker
Armstrong Cork Company
Lancaster, Pennsylvania

Douglas E. Norberg
Howard S. Wright Development Co.
Seattle, Washington

James W. Pattillo
University of Notre Dame
South Bend, Indiana

Carl R. Remington
Porter Paint Company
Louisville, Kentucky

Hadley P. Schaefer
University of Michigan
Dearborn, Michigan

Henry A. Schwartz
IBM Corporation
Armonk, New York

Elliott L. Slocum
Georgia State University
Atlanta, Georgia

Harold M. Sollenberger
Michigan State University
East Lansing, Michigan

Anthony P. Spagnol
The Union Corporation
Verona, Pennsylvania

Leland H. Van Winkle
Varian Associates
Palo Alto, California

Calvin A. Vobroucek
Caterpillar Tractor Company
Peoria, Illinois

Keith E. Willis
Exxon Nuclear
Richland, Washington